HOW TO MAKE A FORTUNE ON THE INTERNET

A guide for anyone who really wants to create a
massive – and passive – income for life

AJAY AHUJA

howtobooks

Published by How To Books Ltd
Spring Hill House, Spring Hill Road,
Begbroke, Oxford OX5 1RX, United Kingdom
Tel: (01865) 375794. Fax: (01865) 379162
info@howtobooks.co.uk
howtobooks.co.uk

The right of Ajay Ahuja to be identified as author of this work
has been asserted by him in accordance with the Copyright,
Designs and Patents Act 1988.

First edition 2007
Reprinted 2007
Reprinted 2009
Second edition 2011

British Library Cataloguing in Publication Data
A catalogue record for this book is available from the British
Library

ISBN 978 1 84528 469 5

Cover design by Mousemat Design Ltd
Produced for How to Books by Deer Park Productions, Tavistock
Typeset by Pantek Arts Ltd, Maidstone, Kent
Printed and bound by Bell & Bain Bain Ltd, Glasgow

NOTE: The material contained in this book is set out in good
faith for general guidance and no liability can be accepted
for loss or expense incurred as a result of relying in particular
circumstances on statements made in this book. Laws and
regulations are complex and liable to change, and readers should
check the current position with the relevant authorities before
making personal arrangements.

Contents

Introduction

I should first tell you what I am not:

- ➤ I am not a computer science graduate
- ➤ I am not an IT consultant
- ➤ I am not a computer programmer
- ➤ I am not a reclusive internet geek
- ➤ I am not computer trained in any way.

The first computer I got was a BBC Micro Model B when I was 13 years old and all I used it for was to play games. All subsequent computers I got were for playing games (even though I convinced my parents they were for my studies!) up until the year 1999.

The computer I got in 1999 was a second-hand office computer which I bought for £200. I had just recently left my full-time job and I had got so used to surfing the internet and emailing my friends at work I couldn't really do without one. I had left my job to pursue a music career, as well as start my own businesses.

By the year 2000 I was using the internet a lot to find investment properties around the UK. I reckon I was one of the first people to use rightmove.co.uk, an estate agency portal where you could conduct property searches and get results made up of all the estate agents registered with rightmove. It would save you a lot of time because you needed to perform the search only once and rightmove would aggregate all the results and display them on one page. Six years on this site has got a Stock Exchange listing valuing the company at over half a billion pounds!

Anyway, back in 2000 I would use rightmove to find hotspot areas to invest in, as I would perform a search for a property based on my criteria (anything under £40,000) and see what came up. When something came up I would visit the area and all the estate agents in that area, including all the estate agents that were not registered with rightmove, and buy everything I could afford. I made a lot of money on the back of this as I would find areas with cheap properties which I would buy, rent out and get a good return on.

Now don't ask me why, but I felt the need to tell everyone what I was doing. It was so simple. I would view a property on rightmove's site, travel to the area, place offers on several properties, raise 100% of the finance with my mortgage broker, buy the properties and let them out. Everything I was buying would rent out and appreciate in value enabling me to buy even more. It was at this point I got the idea of writing a book.

So I got on my computer and composed a letter headed How to Achieve £100,000 p.a. Through Property and I wrote the contents page for my idea for the book in this letter. Then I got on the internet and searched for book publishers. I knew nothing about how to get a book deal, I just thought I would make communication with them and see what happens. I faxed 18 publishers and three responded!

Eventually I did a deal with my first publisher, Lawpack, and in 2001 I wrote my first book about property investment called The Buy To Let Bible. I had no formal writing training. I simply wrote as I spoke. Today it is the best-selling book on UK property investment and is often quoted by property professionals. I'd like to think I have made a few millionaires from people reading my books.

Not content with my first book I contacted other publishers with my idea '147 wake up calls for financial success' and at this point I came in to contact with How To Books, a publisher who publishes books to help people achieve what they want to achieve. They were considering my book idea and after much deliberation How To Books refused to publish it!

The boss of How To Books phoned me up and politely informed me it wasn't for them. I then launched into my sales speech about how I could link the book up to a text messaging service, do this, do that, do whatever so that it would sell. I think the boss liked my sales speech and agreed to squeeze me in between two meetings to talk further.

I met the boss and his wife and we got on. I showed them my ideas and even though they were impressed they still were not convinced. I also mentioned another book idea off the cuff called *The A to Z of Buy To Let Hotspots*. As soon as I mentioned this idea the boss said:

'I'll Have That!'

I was a bit surprised at how quickly he came to that decision since we had been negotiating the butt out of the other original idea. However – who am I to challenge his request for my off the cuff idea! So my second and third books were born:

Buy To Let Property Hotspots and
Property Hotspots in London.

Again, these were a success when they were released. However since the property market was moving so fast the books became outdated very quickly. Then I had an idea. Why don't I create a website that gives the reader a hotspot every month? This meant even though the book went out of date the website would not. And if we promote the website in the book we can get readers to convert into subscribers of the site. So my first site was born in October 2003 called propertyhotspots.net.

Since I knew nothing about computer programming I paid around £4,000 to get the site constructed. It was a members only site and I charged £24.95 for six months' access and £37.95 for 12 months' access. I had no idea how to promote the site, but after a chance conversation with a guy named Adam (who became quite significant further down the line), who I had advised previously about property investment, I learned about Google AdWords.

I will tell you about Google AdWords later in this book, but within two hours of using this system I had my first customer! And then the customers just kept on flooding in. After a few weeks I started thinking that I was selling the site too cheaply so I increased prices to £34.95 for six months' and £49.95 for 12 months' access. But there was no slowing down of customers. So after several price increases the price levelled out to a £20 per month charge. Within four months all development costs had been recouped and I started making a profit.

So by mid-2004 I had confirmed in my mind that you could make money on the internet. My only problem was the cost of bringing new ideas to the internet. If I was facing a £4,000 spend with my internet developers every time I had an idea (which I had many of) then the risk of losing money shot up. This is because I would have to make a major investment each time I came up with an idea and I would have no idea of the outcome. And this was in fact true. The next two ideas I launched flopped and I was roughly £8,000 down on internet development costs.

I realised I needed a cheaper way of creating websites. So I approached one of my friends who worked in IT to construct some sites for me for £200 a go. He did them and I promoted them. The designs were a bit shoddy but they worked and brought in business. The only problem was every time I wanted to change something I had to email him or call him with the amendments and then it would take up to a week before the amendments would be done. And when the amendments were made they were usually wrong anyway!

By late 2004 I was getting really frustrated. It was this frustration that led me to do a Google search for Website Builder which led me to a website which changed my life forever! This is not an overstatement by any means. I dreamt of the possibility of being able to think of an idea in the morning and have it on the internet by night earning money while I sleep. This site enabled me to create a site online simply by dragging the mouse, clicking and typing. Absolutely no coding was required.

So by the end of 2004 I could create my own websites within hours of the inception of the idea. Since then I have been creating sites surrounding a whole number of subjects and I have learnt many tricks, techniques and tactics that have made me a substantial amount of money. I have gone through the trial and error process. I have done the all night sessions, working out where to click, and when, so the sites work. I want to share my experiences with you so that you can skip the learning curve.

Now I will let you know this. You will have to spend around £100 from the outset, around £100 per month ongoing costs and whatever you wish to spend on advertising to get it going if you were to employ *all* the strategies I mention in this book. However you can start with no upfront cost, £10 per month ongoing cost and whatever you want to spend on advertising by doing the bare minimum of what I say in this book. I'll leave that up to you. But I want you to consider doing the former strategy because let's face it: £100 upfront and £100 pm + advertising is *not* exactly a fortune considering what you can expect to get back. If I said to you that you could start a million pound business with a few hundred pounds or thousand pound business with a few pounds – which one would you go for? It's a no brainer really, but I do not know your budget.

About Me

I am male, 34 years old, I live with my girlfriend and I have no children. I work for myself and I have 170 properties worth £13m. I also have my internet businesses which turn over around £1m a year and which are all centered around property investment.

I have written nine books on property investment and I am also a chartered accountant. My interests are simple – business! I've tried other pastimes but they just don't give me a thrill like business does.

How this book works

Consider this book as a manual. You need this manual at your side to refer to while you sit at the computer and use my site www.MassiveAndPassive.co.uk (password: ahuja). Every site I refer to will be accessible from this site so you do not need to remember any individual website other than my one www.MassiveAndPassive.co.uk.

To keep this site exclusive to my readers the site is password protected. To enter the site you need to type in the following code in the password box:

ahuja

That's my surname all in lower case. Then you will be taken to a member registration page where you fill out your name, email address, create a login and password. Remember your login as you will need this to log back in to the site.

So how do you do it?

There are many ways of making money on the internet. I can tell you the way I did and still currently do, but do not assume this is the only way to do it. My formula is thus:

1. Get an idea.
2. Register the name and build the website.
3. Develop products and services list to sell (optional).
4. Get traffic.
5. Capture emails and send newsletters.
6. Add adverts.
7. Sell other people's stuff.
8. Make site sticky (add latest news, chat, forums, video messaging and autoresponders).
9. Get others to sell your stuff.

1. **Get an idea** - you've got to get an idea to kick start this all off. There needs to be a subject or theme your website follows so visitors will spend more than two seconds there. I can help you determine the topic but I can't tell you what to do as I am not you! You need to determine

this for yourself as it is your interest in a particular subject that will see the idea through.

2. **Register the name and build the website** – once you've got the idea you need to register the name on the internet. You've got to give it a name followed by a .com or .co.uk etc. I will show you how to do this. I will also show you how to build a professional looking site in hours. No programming, coding or anything that looks technical is required from you. Just pointing, clicking and typing!

3. **Develop products and services list to sell (optional)** – if you choose to offer a product or service I will show you how to write a sales page so that visitors to your site become customers. I will also show you how to create professional looking eBooks which you can sell for whatever you want. Most eBooks sell for around £47!!!!

4. **Get traffic** – a science in itself! I will show you how to get traffic to your site from major search engines like Google, Yahoo!, Ask, MSN and other major search engines.

5. **Capture emails and send newsletters** – this is a must. I will show you how to extract someone's email from them by enticing them with free gifts if they sign up. Then you can email them whenever you want, directing them back to your site so they click, interact or buy!

6. **Add adverts** – add text ads to your site so that when anyone clicks on them you get paid! I know of web publishers who earn £100,000 per month from this alone.

7. **Sell other people's stuff** – it's called affiliate marketing. You add a link from the seller on your site and every time someone clicks through to the seller's site and buys – you get paid!

8. **Make site sticky (chat, forums, video messaging and autoresponders)** - make visitors stay and come back to your site by making them interact with each other. This is one of the best ways to build online communities. Also I will teach you how to send up to 365 automatic emails when a visitor signs up to your 'auto response service'.

9. **Get others to sell your stuff** - this is called building your own affiliate program. As you sell products for others you get others to sell your products. I know of one website that has 70,000 resellers of their products and they make millions on the internet.

The hardest parts of the whole formula are parts 1 and 3. And they will always be in business. It's products and services that are born from ideas that sell, *not* websites. Websites are just a medium through which you can display your products and services. The rest is just procedure.

Please note that part 3 is optional. Which means you do not have to create anything, it just means you become a seller of other business' products and services. However you still need to know which products and services to sell which should be determined by part 1, your idea.

So let's start with the hardest part first, Chapter 1 – Get an Idea.

1 Get an Idea

Pages to consult in this chapter:

www.MassiveAndPassive.co.uk/get-keywords.html
(password: ahuja)

Now I'm struggling. I'm trying to get an idea of how to stimulate you to get an idea! This is very difficult for me to do. The simple reason is – I don't know you. What I can tell you are the elements of a great idea for a website.

i) It has to have a hunger element

The subject needs to evoke some kind of passion. It has to be a subject which you are prepared to research, examine, analyse and make your life! Some subjects might be:

➤ making money

➤ UK and overseas property investment

➤ expensive hobbies like golf

➤ antiques

➤ raising finance/debt solutions

➤ internet marketing

➤ stocks and shares

➤ beauty and cosmetic surgery

➤ marriage, dating and sex tips

➤ science fiction such as Star Trek memorabilia

➤ classic or modified cars

- boating and yachting
- fishing and angling
- hollywood and celebrity gossip
- coin and stamp collections and latest prices
- aeroplane and train spotting clubs
- weight loss
- eBay
- cult or fad stuff like Scientology
- exercise, health and keeping fit
- fashion and clothing
- specific businesses such as farming, car retailing, etc where there are trade journals already in existence
- interior decorating
- casino and card game clubs and tips
- other gambling sites such as horse racing or dogs
- self development and psychology
- religious groups and communities with a fund raising element
- pet sites specific to a type of pet or breed
- student sites to help with coursework
- cooking
- curing illness
- how to be a writer
- infertility
- computer hardware and software
- movies or even a specific movie (I love Scarface!)
- music - fan sites for individual artists
- wedding planning and weddings in general
- parenting and baby sites
- photography.

The list above is probably less than 1% of what you could do and make serious money from if done well.

I always look at what's being advertised on TV or what's selling well in the bookshops to get ideas. Also internet sales of eBooks hold a lot of information as these books are interactive because they have links to other sites. These sites may be paying out well to anyone who is referring them, hence the creation of the eBook and it doing well, because it just could be the subject of the moment.

Using some of the examples above I ask you how hungry is someone to do the following.

- Make enough money to quit their job.
- Have the confidence to approach the opposite sex.
- Obtain the car of their dreams at the right price.
- Become the master at the card game poker.
- Get out of crippling debt.
- Get rid of acne scars or become thin.
- Be a published author.
- Conceive and have their first child.
- To get back stage passes for their favourite band.
- Have the perfect wedding.
- Be healthy so they live longer.
- Have the ultimate stamp or coin in their collection.
- Improve their golf handicap.

Because it is very difficult to quantify these passions in monetary terms mistakes are sometimes made. You need to provide that platform for these companies to make these mistakes in over paying for advertising on your site.

You can see how many people could be potentially interested in your idea by seeing how many people search for words related to your idea. So if you were thinking of doing a site about 'divorce' then visit:

www.MassiveAndPassive.co.uk/get-keywords.html

and type in divorce and you will get the top 100 search terms that contain the word 'divorce' and how many times it has been searched. So if you typed in 'divorce' you will get other search terms like divorce settlement, divorce law, divorce lawyer, get out of divorce, etc and the number of times these search terms have been searched.

In the above example you may stumble across another idea than the original one. So you may have initially wanted to set up a site about Helping People Going Through Divorce but because you found that 'become divorce lawyer' was searched more than the term 'divorce' your idea for a website has changed to How To Become A Divorce Lawyer. So be flexible and keep your eyes wide open.

ii) It has to be in a high value, high margin industry

I have a saying – 'You will not get rich by selling 1p sweets'. Think about it. Even if you sold 1 million of these you would still only pick up £10,000 and you would have a purchase cost as well of say £8,000 (0.8 pence each) so this would equate to £2,000 profit. And it may take you all year to sell 1 million as well! That's an example of a low value, low margin product. Stay away from them at all costs. The only people who make money in this industry are the established players that sell bucket loads to a global market.

High value, high margin products and services are the opposite. Take for example some software I bought over the internet a year ago. It was a piece of betting software which I was experimenting with to make money. The software was cutting edge and was created and designed by a one man band outfit in Russia. I paid £218 for this software. It cost this guy only his time to create this software and he delivers the product to your email. So virtually all of the £218 is profit for him. This is a high value (being greater than £100) and high margin (being greater than 75%) product.

So if he sold ten of these packages a week he would make over £2,000 in a week. Comparing that to selling 1 million 1p sweets to get the same bottom line, I know which industry I'd rather be in!

So why do I say high value, high margin industry? Well it's two-fold.

1. You can get a piece of that margin if the margin is high enough. Take for example the Russian betting software guy. How much do you reckon he would pay for someone to sell his product on a success only? He's got £200 or so profit to play with. So if he offered £100 to someone to sell his product he would still do well as he would make £100 and the seller would make £100. There would be no product cost to the Russian guy as it's an electronic product and no shipping costs because it's delivered electronically by email. So if you were to sell this product for him then you would earn £100. If you write a good sales page (I will teach you how to write a better sales page than the supplier themselves!) then you could sell five, ten, 50 or even 100 copies a week if the market is big enough. Now if you do the maths that's up to £10,000 per week for simply selling someone else's product!

2. High value, high margin industries tend to be very competitive. Everyone wants a piece of the pie. This means that the businesses within them can spend a lot

on advertising. Using the Russian example again, how much do you think the Russian guy can spend on marketing the product and still make a profit? Assuming he makes about £200 profit per sale before marketing then you can safely say he can spend £100 on marketing the product to get one sale.

If he knows that one in 100 people who view his website will buy, and he is willing to spend £100 on advertising, then he knows that he can spend £1 per click to his website and be assured of a sale. If you didn't know, pay per click is big business. It is where an advertiser approaches a well known search engine like Google and they agree to pay Google an amount every time someone clicks on their advert displayed on Google's site.

What I will teach you is how to display ads on your site so that every time someone clicks on the ad you get paid. So for example if you were displaying the Russian guy's advert on your site and someone clicked on it you would get a share of that £1 and it would be paid by Google. And let me tell you there are many businesses paying well in excess of £1 for a click. I have received over £10 just for one click for an advert displayed on my site.

iii) You must add your own slant to it

Some call it its USP, Unique Selling Point. There must be a reason why people join your site and not others. It could be your straight talking, your particular choice in subject, the quality of your product, or simply that your prices are cheaper than the rest. Whatever it is you must have this edge otherwise you will be what is technically known in business as 'stuck in the middle'. This means there is nothing to distinguish you from the rest of your competitors.

The beauty of the internet is that you may hit on a subject that no one else is talking about and this simply could be your USP. The originality of the subject could be what sets you apart from everybody else. So as long as you stick to the subject you will find that the members of your site stay loyal.

I know of a site that is all about house prices and when the crash is going to occur. They started after I launched my property hotspots site, but they have more forum members than me! I would never have guessed that anyone would want to debate something as doomy and gloomy as a house price crash, but they do.

The USP for my sites are that they focus on low value properties. While everyone else is trying to sell you nice new apartments for £250,000 I am at the other end trying to sell you an apartment for £40,000. I have been tempted to stray over to the other side and sell expensive apartments, because the commission is higher and they are easier to sell, but I want to remain true to the core which for me is at the low end as I know you make more money for clients this way. I want to remain long in business so I believe in providing a product that is good, so in my case a property that achieves a healthy profit for the purchaser. The only healthy profit in the more expensive apartments are for the people who sell them, not the people who buy them!

I hope from reading my three pointers above you have already got a shortlist of ideas. I suggest you use the internet to research further whether others are doing what you're thinking about. If they are, have a look at what they do and see if you can do it:

➤ better
➤ differently

➤ cheaper

➤ or all of the above!

If no one is doing it then hooray! You may have just stumbled on a potential profit making niche subject that has pound notes behind it waiting to be claimed by you!

If you still can't think of an idea

If you can't think of one ask someone else! Do you know of someone who is passionate about something? Do you know of someone who has an insane knowledge about a particular subject? You could do a deal where you take his or her knowledge and put it in to a website.

I am doing this exact same thing where I am partnering up with pioneers of certain subjects and asking them for their knowledge in return for a share of the profits. This way you can build a website with very little input from you. As long as the content you get from these partners is of a suitable standard then all you have to do is cut and paste.

So you now have no excuse not to create a website. Let me tell you there are tonnes of ideas out there yet to be put on the internet. I know that sounds a bit far fetched, but it's very true. Once you surf around you'll see the lack of decent common interest sites to join up to. How often have you searched for quite a generic subject and all the results come back with either irrelevant sites or poorly designed ones with lack of true content of any value?

Okay. So you've got the idea, now let's go and create. You may think this is the hard part, but let me tell you – this is the easy part.

2 | Register the Name and Build the Website

Pages to consult in this chapter:

www.MassiveAndPassive.co.uk/name.html
www.MassiveAndPassive.co.uk/website.html
www.MassiveAndPassive.co.uk/free-articles.html
(password: ahuja)

Register the name

So what does that mean? Does it mean you have to go to Companies House, fill out a complicated form and pay lots of money? No! It will take you five minutes and the name will be registered immediately.

Visit www.MassiveAndPassive.co.uk/name.html and I will guide you through how to register the name.

Tips on choosing a name

The name is what someone will see in the address field of your internet browser, i.e. the place where you type the internet address when you wish to visit their site. Other titles for the name of your website are the domain name, the url, the web address or the website. It is the string of characters that start with 'www'.

The name should be easy to remember – how often have you been told about a site by a friend and then forgotten the whole address? You're left wondering:

➤ was it spelt like this or like that

➤ did it have a hyphen or dot between each word

➤ was it a .com or a .co.uk or even a .me.uk?

So try to make it as easy as possible for them. Avoid long complicated words or misspelling of words of three syllables or more if used with other words. Also avoid long phrases.

So:

➤ www.aboutcomputerz.com – people may forget to tell you about the 'z' at the end and also you may not notice the 'z' as it almost reads perfectly until the end, unlike www. carz.com where you notice the misspelling straight away.

➤ www.everythingyouneedtoknowaboutcomputers.com may be a bit too long as you may remember it as www.everythingyouneedtoknowaboutacomputer.com or another variation.

➤ www.everythingabout-computers.com would require someone to communicate that there is only a hyphen between the second and third words which people will forget to say.

➤ www.eyntkac.com standing for Everything You Need To Know About Computers is too difficult to remember, as it will get lost through remembering some other variation and it requires someone to think of the beginning letters of a seven-word phrase in which errors will occur.

➤ Don't get obsessed by a .com ending. These are the most desired extensions, but that is all it is. .net, .biz, .co.uk and .org are all well respected extensions which are regularly used. I reckon a shorter name .net is better than a longer name .com but this is just my personal opinion.

> If possible try to communicate what the site will be about through the name. So www.eyntkac.com means nothing but a collection of seven letters in no memorable sequence. However www.fixcomputer.net does mean something.

Try performing a search for available names for a site about computers:

Computerz.org.uk
Aboutcomputers.uk.net
fixcomputer.biz
About-computers.co.uk

These were all available when I performed the search on 10 February 2011 and I think they are all good names to use. I quite like the last one as a .co.uk is a well used extension and there are no mispellings.

So go to www.MassiveAndPassive.co.uk/name.html and bear in mind what I have said above.

If you do not require a .co.uk, .org.uk or .biz then you can register your name within the website builder below. If you're a bit new to all this I suggest you register the name within the website builder as it's a lot easier to set your site up. So read on!

Build the website

To build the website visit:

www.MassiveAndPassive.co.uk/website.html

This is an online website builder where you can build your website with unlimited pages. It's the site that did change my business life back in 2004. The site hasn't really changed much. I've found others, but none really match the functionality and unlimitedness of this one. You can virtually do it all with this website creator.

There is a field box to fill in the name of your website. Fill in any name (as we will be assigning your domain name later) and then click on 'Create a website for free>>' and they will look after you from there. If you can point and click a mouse then you can build a website. It's as simple as that. This website builder is extremely user friendly and requires no technical knowledge or ability. Like I said in the beginning I am not a computer science graduate. I am just a guy who wants to make money and I want to do this as easily as possible.

The basics of linking pages together

To link two pages together you have to create what are known as hyperlinks. To link some text to another page on your site log in to your website creator account and go to website/edit/pages, click on 'edit' next to any page then:

1. Type some text and highlight the text you want to link.
2. Click on the icon that looks like ∞.
3. Click on the page that you want to link to that appears in the list in the pop-up page.
4. Click on save page.

To link to a page that is not part of your website do all the same steps above apart from 3, where you simply type in the address of the page you want to link to found in the address bar of your browser in the pop-up page.

Once you've had a play with the website builder and got to grips with it I want you bear in mind these pointers.

Choosing the design

Don't get too hung up on the design. If in doubt always go for the plainer design. There are quite a few designs to choose from. Try to go for a design that isn't too American looking (unless you are aiming for the American market of course) and avoid pictures of goods like cars or computers as they will date your site. Pictures of people always look better than out-dated products.

Background

Always aim for a white background. It's easy on the eye, it's what the big professional sites do and it just looks neater. There are occasions when other background colours are applicable, such as dark colours for spooky or secretive sites, or bright colours if it's for children, but in general if you're talking about a normal subject then keep it normal!

Do not have the background as a repeated graphic image. This just looks tacky, unprofessional and looks like you care more about the design rather than the content. Remember – your website is not your new found art project for you to display to the world! The background images just distract the reader and interfere with the text. In my time I have actually seen moving background images – yuk!

Colour of font

Black, black and black! If you've gone for a white background then this is the optimum colour to use. This is because it is what we are accustomed to see. It's normal, just like if we were reading a book, newspaper or letter.

If you've gone for a non-white background then go for a colour that is opposite to the background colour. This ensures that the text stands out and this is what they have gone to the site for. It is the text that makes your site interesting, not the background. This is why the background is named so – keep the background *in* the background.

Now I have to be honest with you. I'm no good with colours. I dropped my art class at age 13 so I stick with what is generally accepted – black and white! If you want to deviate from this because you think it's boring (there is nothing wrong with being boring you know) then look at what others have done by surfing around on the net. To get a list of the top 500 sites in the UK ranked by most visitors go to www.alexa. com and see what the big sites are doing. Most will be black and white, but there will be other variations to inspire you.

Choice and size of font

Font is the type of text you use. I've generally used Arial font in size 10. I don't know why, it just seems to look nice on the screen. Then I did some research and I found out why I was unconsciously using Arial font. It is one of the two mostly used fonts on the internet. Google, the number one used site on the internet, uses Arial size 10 font. Many businesses use Arial size 10. I suppose I chose this font because others do. But the reason why the big sites use this font is because it's:

➤ the font that is read the fastest
➤ perceived as more legible
➤ considered 'sharper'
➤ the preferred choice when asked
➤ considered a modern font so conveys an image of being up to date
➤ perceived as being sensible so reinforces creditability.

This is based on samples of readers viewing web pages on a standard monitor. Size 12 arial font has been highlighted as the optimum font based on all the studies, but for some reason the general masses have not moved forward with this thinking so I'm not either!

Another font that is used heavily is Times New Roman 12 font. The reason for this is that it has a perceived trust-worthiness and it is a compromise between the old and the new. It has been noted that the serif (the strokes at the end of the lines of the letter) distract the reader and act as noise. A sans serif font (letters that do not have the strokes at the end of the lines of the letters) are easier to read as there is no distraction. Also Times New Roman 12 font is the default font on Word, people start Word documents in this font and only change later so there is a familiarity with this font.

Important: never ever use size 8 font or less. No one will be able to read it! I see a lot of big corporations' sites using size 8 font and it still amazes me. Admittedly it looks nice, but you don't just want a site that looks nice – you want a site that is *useful* to your visitor. These sites may lose visitors because of this, or if it's a site they have to use because of work they'll resent coming to your site as it's just plain difficult to read.

Choice of pages

The number and type of pages is completely up to you. You can have everything on one page (which is surprisingly quite common because all it asks the visitor to do is to scroll down and read the page) or have it split over a logical number of pages. Here's what I suggest and what pages you should include.

1. Home page

This is the most important page. It is the first page readers will see when they type in your domain name. It is this page which will determine whether they will visit any of your other pages. It's your chance (and only chance) to make an impression. You will not get a second chance to do this.

If they like your home page they will stay and find out what you've got to offer by reading further. But if for *whatever* reason they dislike your home page they'll be heading for that address bar ready to type in a new address, clicking the back button, clicking on their default home page or clicking on an ad on your site. They will do whatever it takes to get *off* your site.

You do not want this to happen. So you have to make sure you get your home page right. I will show you how to do this further down the line, but I want you to remember the significance of this page relative to your whole website. This page is damned important and is crucial to your success.

You can stop here and make your home page *the* website. This would work well if you were selling one product and you wanted to spoon feed your sales speech to them with the minimum of interactivity from your potential customer. Lots of eBooks are sold like this. The home page uses clever sales talk so that they press the right buttons in your mind, you eventually press the 'buy now' button and give them your credit card details. Some call it NLP, others call it mind control! Whatever they call it – it works. If you are selling one product then you should consider this strategy.

2. Contact page

A website without a contacts page is just a website. A website with a contacts page is a credible business. It's a website by someone who is willing to put their name, address, telephone, fax and email and sometimes portrait photo to it! I would strongly recommend you put a contacts page on your website with all your contact details on it.

I regularly go from the home page straight to the contacts page to see where they're based, to check if it's an office address, to see if there are any photos of the staff, if they've got a press/PR department or to simply see if they've got a landline and fax number. If there is no contacts page I may click away because I believe that if they do not want to be contacted then their customer service must be lousy.

If you are reluctant to put your actual details, but want readers to be able to contact you, then consider adding a contact form. This is where you create a form of a specified number of form fields and then get the reader to add the data within the fields. This way the communication can be one way and you can respond only if the message is worth replying to. This is better than having no contact details at all.

3. About us page

An about us page is just that. It's a page giving a little history of the website or business or how the whole idea of the site came about. These pages are just nice. They are like the icing on the cake. It gives you a sense of completeness about the site, however this page is not essential. It just shows that you care about the visitor enough to give them a background resumé about yourself and your site.

You can include in your about us page things such as these:

➤ Why you set the site up.
➤ When you started trading.
➤ A brief business history.

➤ CV type information about you and the key staff members.

➤ What your plans are for the business and site.

➤ Your mission statement and plans for the business site.

➤ Key achievements of the business so far.

If you're just starting out some of the things mentioned above may not be applicable, but use the about us page to tell a story about you. Everyone loves a story...

4. Products and services page

If you are deciding to sell a product or service then this is where you showcase your stuff. It all depends on how many products and services you intend to sell and on how you set out the pages, but we will talk about that in Chapter 3.

5. Informational pages

If your site is information based then you need to add these to your site. You must add them in such a way that it is easy to find the information. You should be best placed to know how to split the information up.

If you need content for your site you can get articles to put on it from over 50 free article providers. You can simply cut and paste the article in to your site and display these articles completely free.

Visit:

www.MassiveAndPassive.co.uk/free-articles.html

I will also show you how to add a Google search box to your site, which you can specify to search your site only or the whole web. This way the information on your site can be easily found when specified by the visitor. See Chapter 7 on how to add a Google search box.

6. FAQ - frequently asked questions

This is where you create potential questions and answer them. This is a great page to keep your phone call answering time right down. You need to think of all the questions your readers may have, and then answer them and put their mind at rest. Be honest here. If your product or service doesn't do something that is frequently asked then say so. It will save their time and more importantly yours. On the flipside, if your product does do something that is frequently asked then do say so.

Other pointers you should consider for your FAQs are:

- payment terms
- refund policy
- delivery times
- after sales customer service
- how your product or service works from start to finish
- talk about the features and benefits of your product and service.

Put yourself in the position of a first time viewer of your website and really try to think up potential questions. It's okay to repeat what you have said already on your site to reinforce it in the FAQs. So if you say in your site 'You need no technical knowledge about fishing' it's okay to say:

Q: Do I need any technical knowledge about fishing?

A: No.

This is because the reader may not have read that part in your site and jumped straight to your FAQs, or it's okay to say things twice, thrice or even four times in a different way just to drum a key point into their head.

7. Testimonials

We all love a success story so if you've got one – put it in! People relate to people so if you can show how someone has directly used your product, benefited from it and was kind enough to tell you about it then put it on your site. Testimonials can really work if done correctly. We all look for that testimonial that relates to someone similar to ourselves so we can think 'I'm like him, it worked for him, so why can't it work for me…'.

Do not make testimonials up. They will always sound made up and readers will be able to spot them by a mile. To get testimonials put 'Feedback' somewhere on your site and request their comments back on a contact form or by email.

8. My 'hype it up' pages

So what are my 'hype it up' pages? They're pages that keep visitors coming back to your site time and time again. They are these.

➤ **An autoresponder page** - this is where the visitor gives you their name and email then the page fires off up to seven emails a week automatically for up to a year after signing up. This gives you constant contact with you and the visitor once their email is given. I will show you how to create this page in Chapter 9 - Make Your Site Sticky.

➤ **A chat room page** - this is where visitors can chat to other visitors live on your site about whatever they like. Some visitors have been known to stay chatting on my sites for over six hours! It was also one of the secrets of success for Yahoo! I will show you how to add a chat room to your site in Chapter 9.

➤ **A newsletter page** - a bit like the autoresponder page where you ask for their email to send them your regular newsletter which is updated on your site on a regular basis. I will show you how to do this in Chapter 6.

- ➤ **A forum page** - this is a page where visitors can leave messages or ask questions on the site and other visitors can respond so a dialogue starts going. It's like a chat room except it's not live, so you can post messages and responses come in over time which you can also respond to. I will show you how to do this in Chapter 9.

- ➤ **Latest news page** - this will have all the latest news surrounding your industry or subject. This page will automatically update when a story is reported. It truly is amazing that you can have a latest news page with absolutely no input from yourself! I will show you how to do this in Chapter 9.

- ➤ **A video forum page** - this is where visitors can leave an audio or video message. This is the latest in forums and I will show you how to add this page to make your site look really up to date. I will show you how to do this in Chapter 9.

It is these pages that will set you apart from other websites as I see very few sites that do all of what I suggest above. And the fact is you can do this without having to write one piece of programming code at all!

Assigning your name to the website

If you registered a name under www.MassiveAndPassive. co.uk/ name.html then read on. If you haven't registered a name go to the section 'If this sounds like too much hassle for you' below.

In the first part of this chapter I told you how to register your very own name. Now we have to assign it to the website you have been creating. To do this log in to the website builder account and:

1. Click on 'manage domains' midway on the left hand side of the screen.

2. Then click on 'Add an external domain'.

3. Make a note of the primary and secondary nameservers. They will be the string of words starting with ns1 and ns2. We will need to type these in later so keep a note of them.

4. Log in to the name provider where you registered the name found at www.MassiveAndPassive.co.uk/name.html

5. Go to 'manage domains' and click on 'modify domains'.

6. Then click on 'change nameservers' and add the ns1 string of words obtained in action 3 in the nameserver 1 field and ns2 string of words in nameserver 2 field and then click on 'change nameservers'.

7. *Wait 48 hours*. It takes up to 48 hours for the nameserver changes to take place.

8. Log back in after the 48 hours to your website builder account. Click on 'manage domains' and then 'add external domain' and enter your domain name where it says 'Enter domain name' in the blank field without the 'www'. So if you registered www.myfavouriteplace.com then just add myfavouriteplace.com.

9. Click on 'add domain'.

10. Now your website will appear every time someone types in your website name.

If this sounds like too much hassle for you...

You can register a name within the website builder, but all they offer you are the following: extensions:

.com

.net

.org

You cannot register a .co.uk, .org.uk or a .biz but if this is not an issue for you then it would be simpler to do it within the website builder. They also offer it for *free* as part of the subscription.

When logged in:

1. Go to 'manage domains' then click on 'register a new domain'.
2. Enter the name you want and then click on 'check this domain name'.
3. When a name is available click on the name that you want. It will be either the .com, .net or .org. If they're all available go for the .com first, the .net second and the .org third.
4. Wait 48 hours for the domain to go live for your site.

3 | Develop Products and Services List to Sell (Optional)

Pages to consult in this chapter:

www.MassiveAndPassive.co.uk/informational-products.html
www.MassiveAndPassive.co.uk/accept-payments.html
(password: ahuja)

Notice I say optional. You do not need to create a product or service at all. You can just sell other people's stuff and earn a commission. I show you how to do this in Chapter 8 – Sell Other People's Stuff, but there is plenty to learn in this chapter about general internet marketing so *do not skip this chapter.*

This chapter is effectively split into two parts and the clues are in the chapter title:

1. Development (of products and services)
2. Selling (of products or services).

1. Development

Product development

Let me tell you about the products I sell on the internet.

➤ eBook on how to evict non-paying tenants for £127.95.

➤ eBook on how to sue someone for £9.97.

➤ eBook on how to invest in property for £205.62.

➤ Monthly subscription to property hotspot information for £79.99 per month.

➤ Weekly subscription to the 40 cheapest properties found for sale on the internet for £5 per week.

➤ eBook on property licensing for £47.

➤ Special investors report about investing in the USA for £149.

Now all of these are electronic products. They are informational products that have all been written by me and are available for immediate download. If you can write then you can develop electronic informational products to download! I sell the following:

➤ **eBooks** - eBooks are just the electronic version of a physical book. So if you wrote 'Once upon a time blah blah blah....' in Microsoft Word or any other word processor then this would be an eBook. If you can send a data file via email that has words in it then this data file is an eBook.

➤ **Weekly and monthly subscriptions** - if you can provide information on a daily, weekly or monthly basis that is deemed useful then you can charge for it. There are many subscription sites. I sell property investment information, others sell credit data, pictures, self help videos, dating contacts, classified adverts, auction data, price information, etc. Information that can assist people in making money usually works quite well.

➤ **Special reports** - this is like an eBook but it doesn't have the normal contents and chapters. I define special reports as anything other than an eBook. It's information you want to sell as a one-off hit that you deem to be of value to someone else. So my report about the USA is my research about a certain area and why you should invest in it.

I love selling these types of products because:

1. There is no stock cost as they cost nothing to make other than just your time.
2. They take up no space other than just on the hard drive of your computer.
3. There are no delivery costs as you can send them by email or let users download them from your site.
4. The sale happens automatically with no human input. If someone chooses to buy your product (I show you how to convince them to buy further on) they can get it from you with just a few clicks and the website sends them the product automatically. So it really can be a cash cow chucking out money in to your bank account.

There is no need for any warehouses, overdraft facilities, employees or packaging. It all happens automatically.

So I ask you:

➤ What do you know that someone else would find useful? Useful enough to pay for?

➤ Do you have a particular skill, tip, trick, nack or know-how about a certain subject?

➤ Have you learnt something that you are quite sure no one else knows and could help people in whatever they do?

➤ Can you write software programs that can save a user's time?

There are so many things you can write about and this book is not about telling you what to write. As explained in Chapter 1 you need to get an idea and then the product you decide to develop will be obvious.

To make professional looking informational products visit:

www.MassiveAndPassive.co.uk/informational-products.html

Non-electronic products are basically physical products. I do not actually sell any physical products because my business does not tend to it, but the sort of physical products that are commonly sold by start-up internet companies are:

➤ books, DVDs, games and CDs
➤ electronic products with selling prices from £5 to £299
➤ hobbies, interest and accessories products
➤ clothing, jewellery and other personal items
➤ computing equipment
➤ antiques
➤ toys.

Most internet start-ups usually buy in from a wholesaler and sell on at a profit. My friend Adam, who taught me a lot about the internet, buys his products from Canada and sells them in the UK, Germany and New Zealand. It's a great way to start a business as your product is already there – you've just got to sell it! If the product is a good one then it should sell itself. However just because it's an easy way to start doesn't mean it will work. The product could be so good that everyone is selling it and you'll just be joining the queue!

Another friend of mine actually makes the jewellery items and sells them direct to the public via her website. So the number of items sold will be restricted by how many pieces she makes unless she hires in staff to do what she does. But on the flipside her pieces of jewellery are unique so she has no worry of direct competition as long as her pieces remain sufficiently unique.

So you can do it either way – you can buy in the product or create the product from scratch. It all depends on your idea for your website. You could even do both. You could make your own products and buy in and sell on other products.

Services development

Let me tell you about the services I sell on the internet.

- An eviction service where we send out all the legal forms in connection with evicting a non-paying tenant.
- An accountants referencing service where we issue references in 24 hours.
- Thirty-minute and 60-minute consultations with me about property investment.
- Determination of whether someone needs a property licence and the obtaining of a licence if someone needs one.
- The sourcing of profitable investment properties for people who do not have the time or skill to do so for themselves.
- Buying trips to areas where profitable property investments exist.
- Refurbishment of investment properties for a fixed price.

Now I am able to provide these services because I am suitably skilled to due to my experience in the relative industries. So can I ask you:

> Do you get asked by your friends or family to do something like fix their mobile phone or toilet etc that you could actually charge for?

> Can you teach people a certain skill that you possess which other people desire to have?

> Do you have access to contacts that can provide a service which you can add a commission to?

> Are you qualified in a professional trade where you can get extra customers by promoting this service on the internet?

One of my friends, Chris, is a dab hand at fixing computers. He just loves fixing computers. He gets some kind of buzz out of making something seemingly dead come alive. He has a website explaining his service of fixing computers that do not work which gets him customers in a 15-mile radius of where he lives.

Another friend of mine, Mandip, has a website about evicting tenants for private landlords. She works as a housing officer for a housing association and she knows eviction laws inside out. So in her spare time she does all the paperwork involved in evicting tenants and gets all her clients by promoting her service on the internet. She also helped me kick start my eviction service too!

Again, the services you develop will be as a result of the idea you have decided to pursue as determined in Chapter 1. I hope my and my friends' examples help stimulate your brain to come up with some creative and innovative products and services.

Once you come up with the products and services you then need to sell them.

2. Selling

A business is nothing without a sale – it's simply an idea. So you need to make sure you get your selling process right. The amount of great products and services I see that never result in a sale amazes me. The creators believe that the product is so great that it doesn't need to be sold – *wrong!* This may be true for established products and services, but for every new product or service it needs a 'sales pitch'.

> ### My indisputable rule:
> No matter what market you sell to, your product or service *needs* to have a *superb* sales pitch!

Of course, you can put any old rubbish on your website; but if you want a sales pitch that actually entices your visitors to *buy* your product or service, you need to make sure you're using copywriting techniques that proven to produce results; results that will earn you cash!

I know how effective this needs to be, because I've been selling on the internet for over three years, in which time I have learnt what works and what doesn't. If I knew then what I know now then I reckon I would have earned over £1m more in sales, but hey I can't complain!

I have been using a formula on my own websites which I want to share with you. I have quadrupled my sales over the last two years by using my tricks which I have learnt through experience and other internet marketers. It's true, the *way* you sell it determines how many of your products and/or services you're going to sell; and ultimately how much cash you're going to rake in.

In this chapter I'm going to show you the three critical elements that will help you structure your sales pitch and how to test what you create to see if it's working. The more you refine your sales pitch the better it will work.

There are elements of a sales pitch which even a child could understand. That's the beauty of sales. We all understand it on an instinctive level as we have all been sold to.

Fact:

A brilliantly thought out sales pitch can potentially *rocket* your sales!

People fundamentally sell over the internet because you have the chance to communicate with *millions* of people, a target audience previously untouchable. Conversely, you don't have the opportunity to *meet* these potential customers in person to tell them why your product or service is exactly what they're looking for. It sounds simple, but it's a fact, you need to *sell* something to someone before you can even think about gaining the sale.

Your sales pitch will do this for you, if you follow these techniques:

➤ A brilliant sales pitch posted on your website will build trust and highlight how what you are selling will benefit the consumer. In a nutshell **your sales pitch is your top salesperson** so treat it like one!

➤ Initially you need to identify which kind of sales pitch is going to be more suited to what you are selling. Is it a long, descriptive pitch (greater than 750 words) or a short, punchy pitch?

Long sales pitch

I've had many a debate with other website owners about whether a long sales pitch works and most agreed with me that it does. I've tested it time and time again to ensure that what I have is going to *sell*. I've used it on my own websites to make *a fortune* in online sales!

If you:

➤ sell a single product or service

➤ sell a product range that is closely linked

then you definitely need a long sales pitch to try to reel your audience in.

Short sales pitch

If your website advertises loads of different products with different product categories, a short sales pitch has proved to be more effective as it's snappier, easier to read and keeps your buyers' interest (which is what's going to make them click the 'buy now' button!).

So determine which category you fall into before you get in to the nitty gritty of writing your sales pitch so you can establish whether you need to write a 750+ word master-piece or several mini wonders less than 750 words.

Writing your sales pitch

Once determined there are five elements you should be aware of when writing your sales pitch which keep you well ahead of your competitors.

I have used all or some of these elements on my website to boost my sales. Websites I create now use *all* of the techniques below because I know they work as I've reaped the benefits. The techniques may seem obvious but, it's the obvious stuff that often gets overlooked. We sell to people as we've been sold to before. The five things you have to do to get the sale are:

1. Write to your target audience.
2. Write an exciting headline.
3. Make them believe you can solve their problem.
4. Talk about the benefits as well as the features.
5. Ask for the sale.

1. Write to your target audience

You have to define your audience beyond simply 'people on the net'. You must know *exactly* who the people are that will buy your product or service and then target your sales pitch to precisely what they're looking for.

So you've got to ask yourself – who is my target audience?

➤ What gender are they?
➤ How old are they?
➤ What is their education level?
➤ What problems do they face?
➤ Can you offer your product/service as a viable solution?

If you don't know or have an indication of the answers to the above questions, you need to go back and do a little bit more research. All of this is pivotal to making your effective sales pitch.

Once you've got an idea of who they are then write to them in a style that they will understand and that connects with them. So for example if it's for teenagers keep it current and less formal and if it's for professional business people keep it more formal.

2. Write an exciting headline

Headlines are key. The *most* effective headlines promise an answer to the problem your visitor has arrived on your site trying to solve.

Take a look at these eye-catching headlines from two of my websites.

From my www.samedayreferences.co.uk:

> **"Get an Accountants Reference *within 24 hours* sent <u>direct</u> to your chosen lender or get <u>200%</u> of your money back!"**

and from my other site www.phpremier.co.uk:

> **"Earn up to £2,000 per month profit by *owning* and <u>*renting*</u> out an exclusive central London property. Prices start from only £150,000 and did I mention you get a 441% return on your money in 3 years!"**

compare that to: 'Welcome to my site' or 'Invest in London for immediate profit'.

So have an exciting headline in speech marks in size 18+ font which explains what the reader could expect to get if they read on further. Keep your headline **relevant, simple, and to the point**. This will encourage your potential customer to keep reading! The better the headline, the more people who will read on, the more people who will (with the right sales pitch) consider buying and ultimately the more people who *will* buy!

I would use underline, italics and bold on the key words to emphasise what you are promising because it acts as a trigger to keep them reading on. Bold, italic and underline act as mini bolts to keep the reader's interest and combined with the large font makes the headline almost shout at you!

If you can hit 'em with a good opening headline then 25% of your work has been done.

Also when you write the body of the text try to break the blocks of text up with:

➤ Complete lines of space so the paragraphs are separate rather than separated by indentation only
➤ Short paragraphs
➤ Using bold, italics and underline for key parts of the sales pitch
➤ Highlighting the key parts of the text with a colour behind it
➤ Using tables, boxes and speech mark quotation like snippets.

Do whatever you can just to keep the reader reading. You'll be amazed at how quickly we get bored with reading paragraphs of text all of the same size, font and decoration if we are not sure if the text will be beneficial to us. We all follow the motto 'if in doubt bail out!' because we just don't have the time to really find out if the text is useful in any way. This is why you have to spoon-feed what you are saying to them by using a few frills.

3. Make them believe you can solve their problem

You need to earn your potential customer's trust...and quick! When using websites you cannot afford to have long spiels about irrelevant experiences you've had etc – you need to establish your credibility for what you're saying straight away.

Tell them what you've achieved in the past

Are you fully qualified in the area you are selling? Written any published works relating to it? Any *positive* media publicity you've received? If so, put it in – it will all help!

Relate to your potential customer

Is your potential customer's problem one you once faced? Are you now offering them a solution as a direct result of an experience? Tell them if that's the case and tell it in a story fashion – as I've said before everyone loves a story.

Gather and use testimonials

People want to know that other people have used your product and benefited. When it comes to using your customers' feedback in your sales pitch you have to get the right blend of specificity and punch: not all testimonials are created with equal punch.

This is one testimonial received after the customer used my www.fastlet.com service:

> *Fastlet offers a high quality, efficient service which far outstrips any of the major high street bathroom and kitchen installers. And on top of all this the total price for bathroom installation and tiling was by far the most competitive I could find. My only regret is that I didn't use Fastlet to refit my kitchen. I will have no hesitation in recommending Fastlet to anyone in the future.*
>
> **Sam Rothwell, East London**

The most effective testimonials highlight the benefits and results your customers have achieved after buying your product or service, so potential customers will see that you *deliver* what you say you will. If you haven't got a testimonial then ask for one! If you can give your product away then do so in exchange for a testimonial (and make sure you get a good one!).

Add a strong guarantee

A strong guarantee shows you stand behind what you're selling. This will reduce your potential customers suspicions and increase their chances of buying from you.

Take a look at my www.samedayreferences.co.uk service highlighting the guarantee:

> **"...within 24 hours sent direct to your chosen lender or get 200% of your money back!"**

By offering this guarantee you are giving credibility to your service and making a promise that appears too expensive for you not to fulfil!

4. Talk about *benefits* as well as the features

Do you know the difference between a feature and a benefit? Let me enlighten you.

A feature is something specific to the product or service. So for example a TV being able to display images in colour has the feature of being colour.

A benefit is something the user actually receives from the feature. So in the colour TV example the benefit for the user is that they get to see a more true to life image than a black and white TV.

Be sure to always include the benefits as well as the features. So for example:

➤ **Feature:** super concentrated washing up liquid for intensive cleaning.

➤ **Benefit:** eat off cleaner plates and get them clean in half the time leaving you to do the things you really want.

➤ **Feature:** electric windows with child safetly sensors.

➤ **Benefit:** get peace of mind knowing that your child never risks serious injury.

I source profitable investment properties for clients so if I were to write keywords relating to the features and benefits of my service my worksheet may look like this:

Features	Benefits
Profitable	Saves you time
We negotiate for you	Handhold you through the process
Use my expertise	No need to get your hands dirty
Access off the market deals	Get the job done correctly
Use my existing reliable solicitors, brokers, letting agents	Provides secure retirement income
	Peace of mind

Then I would include the above features in my website and emphasise the benefits that my service brings to them, hoping along the way I would connect with them through my sales pitch so that they pick up the phone to call us or email us for further information.

5. Ask for the sale/order!

OK, so you've got your potential customer's attention and hooked them through the sales pitch by explaining the features and benefits of your product or service. So what now…ask for the order and turn them from that *potential customer* I've referred to into a paying customer!

You have to make clear exactly what they have to do to get your product or service. I have seen many a sales pitch fall at this final but most crucial hurdle. They do not ask the reader to do anything. They assume the reader will look to the left menu bar and see the phrase 'order now' but readers don't! Only if your product is so damned good that they're itching to buy your product because they have heard about it from someone else (in this case you wouldn't even need a sales pitch!) would they even hunt around for the 'order now' button.

So in your site have the sentence which explains to them exactly what they have to do. So for example:

To book your appointment, please click the 'buy now' button below!

Click here to take advantage of this limited offer!

To get your reference with our 200% money-back guarantee – call this number now…!

But it doesn't stop there. If you add a sense of urgency to the sale then this doubles the response. I add words to the effect of:

There are only 50 copies left at this price so order now…

Order before 31st December…and benefit from the specially reduced price of £x

If you order before the end of October you will get my free gift worth £299 as a special bonus.

Asking them for the order and letting them know they will get some kind of special price or free gift if they act now encourages them to buy now rather than miss out on the chance.

So in summary the audience, headline, credibility, benefits and features and asking for the order are the five essential elements you need on your website in order to make *a fortune*. Add these using the techniques explained and you'll create a top salesperson working 24/7 with no salary costs!

Make sure you care about the presentation and image of your product or service as much as you do about the sale of them – constant review and analysis will breed results and results mean *money*!

When it comes to your business on the net, your own sales pitch is unique to you and the only chance you have to communicate directly with your potential customers, telling them *why* they should buy from you as opposed to someone else.

Not many websites use these five critical elements and as such you're *already* one step ahead of the game just by making sure your copy includes the essential elements discussed here! There are not a lot of people using the internet in the UK to make *a fortune* so your destiny is in your own hands. By testing the different parts of your sales pitch regularly you'll know how well your site is performing and what, if anything, needs to be changed to prevent potential sales from going down the drain.

Accepting payments

This is real easy. Visit: www.MassiveAndPassive.co.uk/accept-payments.html and there you will be directed by the payment processor to sign up giving the normal sign up details.

Once this is done you simply add your email and password for this new account in the e-commerce section of the website creator and then you're ready to add your products and services to the web shop.

I will teach you how to add products to your web shop at my site www.MassiveAndPassive.co.uk.

4 Get Traffic

Pages to consult in this chapter:

www.MassiveAndPassive.co.uk/Google-AdWords.html
www.MassiveAndPassive.co.uk/worksheets.html
www.MassiveAndPassive.co.uk/get-keywords.html
www.MassiveAndPassive.co.uk/conversion.html
www.MassiveAndPassive.co.uk/other-ppc.html
(password: ahuja)

So what does 'get traffic' mean? It's all about visitors. You need people to get to your site. There are three ways you can let people know about your website.

1. By word of mouth.
2. By offline media.
3. By online.

Two out of the three ways above are a complete waste of time when it comes to promoting a start-up website. All three may work for other types of start-ups, but for websites only one works – do you know which one?

Well I'll stop you guessing – it's number three, online. The reasons why one and two don't work and number 3 does is because of the following.

1. Word of mouth advertising

Website names get lost in translation. All the easy to remember words as names such as house.com, cars.com, money.co.uk etc have gone. When you start to add words to these generic words then people forget. So if you found this site called www.go-money.co.uk and told someone about it eight times out of ten it will be remembered as something else such as gomoney.com, gomoney.co.uk or some other variation. Or if you see a website called www.jooby-dooby.com which has no meaning you will find it diificult to remember. Statistics show that the average number of times someone retypes an address if the first one isn't the one they are looking for is two!

So statistically you've only got three chances to get that visitor. But this all depends on someone actually acting upon someone else's recommendation of your website. How many times have you been given a recommendation of a website and either forgotten what it is or never acted on it anyway? Again statistics show it's around nine out of ten times you either forget or have no interest in visiting the site.

So equating the likelihood of someone:

➤ hearing about your site and actually being interested in visiting it
➤ remembering to look you up
➤ remembering your actual domain name
➤ retyping your name until they get it correct

and actually landing at your site is pretty slim. Some will find their way to your site, but there are too many things that can go wrong, or simply not occur, for them to actually end up at your site which make word of mouth promotions ineffective.

2. Offline media advertising

This is basically any media that is not online: newspapers, magazines, radio, TV, posters, etc. This is slightly more effective than word of mouth as a viewer/reader can actually see the domain name in print or on the screen so the likelihood of a mistype is lowered. However it still requires the viewer/reader to go to their computer and type the address in.

It has been shown that unless the viewer/reader is at the computer at the time they see the ad you have only a one in ten chance of them actually visiting your site *if* they were interested in your advert in the first place. This in my books is a very poor statistic. And considering that advertising in any sort of well known newspaper, radio station or TV channel can cost a small fortune the return on marketing investment is extremely low.

Offline media advertising can work if it is alongside other promotions for larger corporations which are trying to promote a brand rather than a direct product. Since you are going to be a small fish in a very big pond offline advertising is not for you unless it is completely free and does not take up too much of your precious time.

3. Online advertising

For someone to visit your site all they need to do is *click*. That's it. No remembering or retyping of domain names because all the reader needs to do is see your advert, link or image and if they like it they will click and – bang; they're at your site.

Now this all assumes they have the internet so they are able to click. But without sounding obvious your customers should only be people who have access to the internet! If you are aiming your site at someone who should love your idea so much so that they badger their son, daughter, friend or work collegue to show them the site because they do not know how to use the internet then you are using the wrong platform to promote your idea.

It's like if you were advertising a plasma TV over the TV networks such as ITV, Channel 4 or Sky, you can safely assume that the viewers have at least a TV otherwise they would not be able to view your advert. So you can safely say that the viewer could at some point be interested in the TV that is being advertised because they *have* a TV. It's the same with websites. If you promote a website on someone else's website you can assume that the reader of someone else's website could be interested in your website because they are actually able to view your website because they have a computer! Do you catch my drift?

There is no need to try to convert people to the internet. Let Tesco, Amazon or whoever else that has billions do this. All you want are people who have regular access to a computer with an internet connection and use it. So advertising by methods 1 or 2 may create interest in your site, but will not actually result in any visitors to your site. If you have no visitors then no matter how great your site looks *it's not a website – it's a painting*!

Hopefully you'll agree with me that the *only* way to promote your website is online. So how do you do it online? You do it on a little known site called 'Google' using their clever program Google AdWords.

Google AdWords

Google allows you to display a small three-line advert on the right hand side of their page when someone searches for a search term that you have specified. It's called The Google AdWords Program. If the searcher sees your advert and clicks on it they will land on your home page and

Google will charge you anywhere from 1p to your maximum price, which you can specify.

How Google AdWords works

Have you ever heard of the expression 'being at the right *place* at the right *time*'?

This old expression is quoted by anyone who knows of anyone that has made a lot of money from a simple deal.

This is what Google AdWords is all about.

➤ The **place** is Google.co.uk.

➤ The **time** is when *your* ad is displayed.

> This is how commercial land owners, newspapers or market organisers have profited before. Anyone wishing to earn an honest living pays a landlord rent, a newspaper advertising fees or a council rent and/or rates so they can showcase their stuff.

Guess what? – Google is the *new* landlord and newspaper!

➤ Google landlord - this landlord is different. He lets you rent for free. He lets you set up shop and only charges you for when a customer enters your shop (i.e. when the user clicks on your advert)! Can you imagine that? A landlord that lets you have a shop for free, *no rent* or council taxes and no service charges. He only charges you when a customer enters your shop.

➤ Google newspaper - this newspaper is different. He lets you advertise for free. Only ever charging you when a reader *responds* to your advert. Try running that one by the *Sunday Times*!

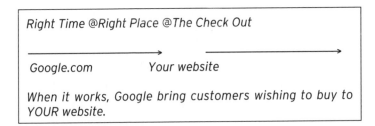

Right Time @Right Place @The Check Out

Google.com   Your website

When it works, Google bring customers wishing to buy to YOUR website.

But it gets even better. The more **relevant** your ad the more likely it is to be 'aired' and the *less* you have to pay. Why?

Well, when Google first started, way back in 1998 (which was only nine years ago – a lifetime on the net), they were the first search engine that produced relevant results.

So while Yahoo and AltaVista were search engines *as well as* re-sellers of goods, Google were just damned good result providers. So by 2004 they became the most used search engine because of the way their programs worked.

So Google's USP (unique selling point) was that they were relevant. Relevance is key to the success of any search engine. What is the point of visiting a search engine if all they produce are irrelevant results? So relevance is what they demand from any advertiser also.

- ➤ If you are relevant you do not pay so much.
- ➤ If you're mildly relevant you'll pay heavily.
- ➤ If you are irrelevant you won't pay anything at all as you won't even get shown!

So the key is to be relevant!

Relevance

So how can you be relevant? The best way to be relevant is to *know your customer*. There is a really easy way to know your customer. All you have to do is work out what your customer wants by the way they search.

If you know what they search and all variations of it then your ad will show. With a well written ad you'll get chosen. If you get chosen consistently then you *must* be relevant!

Google have a neat way of deciding on whether you are relevant. It's called the:

click thru rate (CTR).

This means:

➤ if your ad is clicked thru 100 times, every 100 times it is aired your CTR is 100% and you are *very relevant*!
➤ If your ad is clicked thru once every 100 times it is aired your CTR is 1% and you are mildly relevant.
➤ If your ad is *never* clicked thru your CTR is 0% and your ad will get thrown out and won't even get a look in.

Think about it. If you do get clicked thru based on the search term 100 times out of every 100 times you are displayed then you must be very relevant to what is being searched. Google will love you as you follow their mission statement which is:

Google *must* provide *relevant* results.

So if you are following Google's mission statement they feel obliged to reward you. The way they reward you is to charge you *less* the *more* relevant you are. They do this by working out your Google score.

Google score

Your Google score is determined as:

CTR × maximum bid price in pence for a search term
= Google score.

So in the above example (extreme as it is) if you have company A having a maximum bid price of £1 for the search term 'property', and company B having a maximum bid price of £2, and company A having a CTR of 100% and company B having a CTR of 1%, then their respective Google scores are:

Company A: 100% × 100p = 100
Company B: 1% × 200p = 2

So company A has a higher Google score than company B. So even though company B is willing to pay £2 per click company A still ranks higher and pays only £1 for the click.

But it gets even better! All company A has to do to beat company B is get a score greater than 2. If they can maintain a CTR of 100% and pay a cost per click of 10p then their score is:

Company A: 100% × 10p = 10

This is greater than company B.

So even though company B is willing to pay £2 per click and company A is only willing to pay 10p, company A still gets ranked *higher*.

Cost per click

So in this extreme example company A pays only 10p and gets ranked first. So what does company B pay? Well Google have another rule:

You only pay 1p more than the next highest bidder

So if you introduce company C and company D, who have a click thru rate of 10% and are willing to pay 50p and 5p per click, you have their Google score at:

$$\text{Company C: } 10\% \times 50p = 5$$
$$\text{Company D: } 10\% \times 5p = 0.5$$

So the cost per clicks (known as CPC) are as follows:

Rank position		Google score	Max CPC	CPC
1st	Company A	10	10p	8p
2nd	Company C	5	50p	7p
3rd	Company B	2	£2	6p
4th	Company D	0.5	5p	5p

So companies A, B, C and D can be identified as these following typical companies:

Company	Name	Why?
Company A	The winner	This company knows the value of money *and* relevance. They are playing Google's game. Since Google have earned their position to be the number one search engine they are deciding to play by Google's rules. They have studied how Google's system works and thus worked the system knowing full well they will get rewarded for it.
Company C	The amateur	They have some understanding of being relevant. They know that being relevant costs them less money, but being relevant requires *effort*! So to bypass effort they'll just increase their cost per click to a level they can afford with the hope they'll ppear somewhere on the first or second page.

Company	Name	Why?
Company B	The lazy	This company is stupid. They have *no* idea of being relevant. All they have is a big marketing budget. This budget has been given to an employee who has no understanding of money or ROI (return on investment). This company will spend that marketing budget in *full* but will get very few real enquiries.
Company D	The poor	This company will rarely get their ads viewed as they will be placed on the eigth or ninth page. They can still do well as the type of user viewing the eigth or ninth page will be a serious searcher. They will pay less than 8p per click and generally be start-ups or less established companies.

I have helped many people with their 'pay per click' (PPC) campaigns and most fall into the amateur or the poor category. Very few were in the lazy category because I had very few clients that had budgets of greater than £100,000 per month. But they *all* had one mission in mind: they wanted to be in the winner category.

We all know in life that not everyone can be the winner. To be the winner requires you being better than your competitors. The information below will help you become the winner. I still sell this information below as an eBook for £60 on one of my websites, but I am giving you this for free. It's called '**mastering the art of Google AdWords**'. Most website creators cannot be bothered to master Google AdWords as they do not appreciate how effective it can be. I hope you will not behave like most website creators. However if you're the lazy type then skip this section and read the section in the next chapter called 'The lazy man's guide to Google AdWords'.

5 | Mastering the Art of Google AdWords

First you need to open a Google AdWords account. To do this visit:

www.MassiveAndPassive.co.uk/google-AdWords.html

It's fairly simple to open an account and use. One thing you can always be assured of with Google and that is useability. It's very easy to get your adverts on to Google. I see plenty of badly worded adverts which I am sure never get clicked. If these idiots can use Google AdWords I'm quite sure you can!

The difficult bit is getting them aired enough *and* getting them clicked enough. This is what I want to focus on because this is the difficult bit.

1	2	3	4	5	6	7
Know your customers	Segregate customers	Cater for personalities	Cater for ad types	Write ad	Allocate search terms for each ad group	Test, monitor and revise

Know your customers

In this part forget about me, me, me, it's *you, you, you*! Or to rephrase correctly it's less about you, you, you and more about *them, them, them*! Them being your customers.

Who are the type of people who are willing to *buy* off you? You really need to understand *them*. It's *them* who pay your bills so had you better get to know them. The way to identify them is to know who would want your product or service. If you're selling a property refurbishment service then you can be assured that the following traits exist in a potential customer:

1. They own their own home.
2. They have more than £5,000 in the bank to spend.
3. They earn significantly more than the average salary.
4. They are over 18.
5. They want to enhance their home/assets.

You can also make some wilder judgements like:

1. They have a better sense of the value of money than others.
2. They might run a business on the side as well as being in employment.
3. They are time constrained.
4. They lack the know-how regarding the refurbishment business.

This is a small list. The idea is just to sit back and think about who would actually purchase your product or service. Don't have blind belief that your product is so great that everyone would as the truth is that the majority won't!

'If you send a postcard offering a free six-pack of beer with the purchase of two large pizzas to a list of purchasers of a pay-per-view boxing match (a list which you purchased from your local cable TV company), you are more likely to get a big response than if you sent the same offer to a list of the ladies' auxiliary bridge club.'

Steve Conn, marketing consultant

Steve clearly understood the customer for two large pizzas!

Here's a checklist of prompters that will help you establish some of the traits of your typical customer.

1 Know Your Customers (Worksheet 1)	
Questions	**Answers**
1. What industries surround your product and who do these industries serve?	
2. How much does your typical customer earn?	
3. What job does your typical customer have?	
4. What age group is he or she in?	
5. Are they male or female?	
6. Why have they arrived at your site?	
7. Are they based in a specific region?	
8. What else is your customer interested in?	
9. How intelligent is your customer?	
10. Are they married?	
11. Do they drive?	
12. Do they own a credit card and have good credit?	
13. Do they own their own home?	
14. Are they in a professional trade?	

You can find this worksheet at: www.MassiveAndPassive. co.uk/worksheets.html.

Based on the answers to these questions and more you should be able to create a pool of traits of your typical customer. I'm sorry if this sounds like a marketing diploma, but the diploma is there for a reason (I've never studied for one but they make excellent points!). Once you have a pool of traits we can start building *real people* out of these and start segregating the customers.

1	2	3	4	5	6	7
Know your customers	**Segregate customers**	Cater for personalities	Cater for ad types	Write ad	Allocate search terms for each ad group	Test, monitor and revise

Segregate customers

So we have a whole load of traits – what do we do with them? We can group traits together to build up a typical customer and give them a name. This is probably the most difficult thing to do. It requires really understanding your product and picturing the type of people that would buy your product.

Let's say I was marketing Chapters 4 and 5 about how to get traffic to your website as an eBook. I would need to know my product inside out and I would need to have an idea about my potential customers. Well I know my product and I think I know my customers. Based on my understanding of my product (being these chapters) I have come up with the following customer types for my product of 'how to get more traffic to your website' with their associated motives.

Customer category	Typical customer	Motives	Explanation
Owner	Business person	To increase online profits	This is the most clued up customer you can have. They understand income and expenditure and how they interact with each other. They will carefully evaluate what you are offering and consider what you're offering an investment rather than a purchase.
Part owner	Partner of business or sales director	To increase sales	This person is part of an organisation and is either a partner or director with decision-making powers. They are where they are as they are good at getting sales. This is their main focus. Cost acquisition per customer is something for the accounts department to sort out!
Part-timer	Runs business alongside employment	To reduce costs	This person works and runs a business on the side. They don't have the time to really analyse too much as they work. Time is the limited resource with this person. They will look for a cheap way to promote, to preserve the salary from their employment.
In the industry	Owns a business in the PPC (pay per click) industry	To increase knowledge level	This person works in the PPC industry. It pays to keep ahead of the game. They have a thirst for knowledge about PPC. If they can get just a few tips then it's worth it as they can transfer to this to their customers.

It took me a long time to come up with this. About a day's thinking. But it is important that you do give this part of the exercise some real thought. Use the worksheet opposite to help you.

2 Segregate Customers (Worksheet 2)			
Customer category	Typical customer	Motives	Explanation

You can find this worksheet at: www.MassiveAndPassive. co.uk/worksheets.html.

You need to know who your customer is and why they want to buy your product. So for example if you are a retailer of video games then your customer categories and motives may be as follows.

Customer category	Typical customer	Motives	Explanation
Adult	An adult who plays video games	To get the latest games at the cheapest prices	An adult will want to get the best price as they are parting with the money. They will also want the latest games to be available and they may not know what game to get until they browse the site.

▶

Customer category	Typical customer	Motives	Explanation
Parent	A parent who has a child who plays video games	To get the video game of their child's choice for the cheapest price	A parent will want to get the best price, for a specific game that a child has chosen.
Child	A child who plays video games	To get the video game and the most freebies the site is offering (and instructing their parent to use their credit card)	A child may not be so focused on price, but will want to get extras on top of the purchase.

So you can see that these three customer types are very different with differing motives. We can use these differing motives to construct well targeted ads so we can capture all three types. But before we get to the ads we can further segregate the customer. Read on...

1	2	3	4	5	6	7
Know your customers	Segregate customers	**Cater for personalities**	Cater for ad types	Write ad	Allocate search terms for each ad group	Test, monitor and revise

Cater for personalities

We are not robots. We are all different in our own ways. We have personalities. This becomes a big problem if you're trying to get your customer to respond to you! If I knew your personality then it would be easy to get you to respond. So for example if I know you're a bit of a perfectionist and you think you're ahead of the game then I might run an ad that says:

> *Perfect Your PPC*
> Masterclass in AdWords
> Not For Novices – Join *now*
> www.MassiveAndPassive.co.uk

This ad might work well with you, but not so well with others. If I spent all day thinking up personality types my Google AdWord campaign would take for ever to compile. Since we do not have an unlimited amount of time to compile personality types we have to think of a more base level type.

In my experience in business I meet a lot of business people. There are the formal types and the informal types. They are very different and the difference between them, I think, is enough to further segregate. They respond differently enough which helps me target them differently.

➤ **The formal types** – I picture this customer in a shirt and tie. He refers to his customers as clients, his income as fees and his costs as expenditure. He follows the rules.

➤ **The informal types** – I picture this customer in jeans and a T-shirt. He works funny hours, bends the rules to get the job done and takes bigger risks.

So we can compile our likely set of customers:

Customer category	Personality	Customer type
Owner	Formal	1. Formal owner
	Informal	2. Informal owner
Part owner	Formal	3. Formal part owner
	Informal	4. Informal part owner

Customer category	Personality	Customer type
Part-timer	Formal	5. Formal part-timer
	Informal	6. Informal part-timer
In the industry	Formal	7. Formal in the industry
	Informal	8. Informal in the industry

So we have eight customer types. Now I know my customer types I can try to connect with them as best I can. I will picture each one of these customer types sitting in front of the computer and try to write an ad so they respond.

Think about a base level personality which will help you divide your customer base. Example divisions could be:

➤ male/female

➤ old/young

➤ rich/not so rich

➤ employed/self-employed

➤ homeowner/tenant

➤ professional/not professional

➤ B2B/B2C.

The list can go on. It has to be a sensible division that is relevant to your product or service. You can divide into more than two groups. The more you divide the better understanding of your customer you will have. Example divisions could be:

➤ Salary range 1/salary range 2/salary range 3...

➤ Age range1/age range 2/age range 3...

➤ Geographical region 1/geographical region 2/geographical region 3...

But remember – the more you divide the more ads you will have to write. This will be obvious as you read further.

Number of customer types

So based on this chapter and the last two chapters you will be able to determine the number of customer types. It's simply:

Number of customer categories × number of personalities = number of customer types

So in my case it's 4 × 2 = 8.

Since there are eight different customer types I'm going to have to write eight different ads. Each customer deserves their own ad as each customer type is different as established through the workings above.

But before we start writing the ads we need to learn a little about ad types. Read on...

1	2	3	4	5	6	7
Know your customers	Segregate customers	Cater for personalities	**Cater for ad types**	Write ad	Allocate search terms for each ad group	Test, monitor and revise

Cater for ad types

Here is what Michael Fortin thinks about writing ads.

Michel Fortin is a direct response copywriter, author, speaker and consultant. His speciality is long copy sales letters and websites. Watch him rewrite copy on video each month, and get tips and tested conversion strategies proven to boost response in his membership site at http:// TheCopyDoctor. com/ today.

Article source: http://EzineArticles.com/

When writing direct response copy there are a few things that can maximise the responsiveness of your message. The first and most important element that can turn any website, salesletter or ad into an action-generating mechanism is the headline.

A headline is meant to do two vital things.

First, it needs to grab your reader's attention. Realise that people surfing the web are click-happy. They tend to scan web pages quickly, even many of them simultaneously. Your site is but a blur. So, your headline must be prominent and effective enough to stop them.

Second, your headline needs to pull the reader into the copy and compel her into reading further. To do that, it must cater to a specific emotion or a relevant condition – one to which the reader can easily associate. Here's a list of 'triggers,' coupled with actual examples I used in the past:

- *Curiosity: 'Revealed! Closely guarded secrets for...'*
- *Mystery: 'The five biggest mistakes to avoid by...'*
- *Fear: 'Over 98.4% of people end up broke when...'*
- *Pain: 'Suffering from needless back pain? Then...'*
- *Convenience: 'How to increase your chances with...'*
- *Envy: 'How fellow marketer pummels competitors by...'*
- *Jealousy: 'They all laughed when... until I...'*
- *Sloth: 'Slash your learning curve by 57% when...'*
- *Love, lust: 'Make her fall in love with you with...'*
- *Shock: 'Finally exposed! Get the dirty truth on...'*
- *Greed: 'Boost your income by more than 317% when...'*
- *Pride, power, ego: 'Make fellow workers squirm with...'*
- *Assurance: '...In less than 60 days, guaranteed!'*
- *Immortality: 'Reverse the aging process with...'*
- *Anger: 'Banks are ripping you off! Here's why...*

*By the way, most of these headlines were enormously
successful for my clients, not because they were tested
and tweaked (and most of them were), but because they
were actually stolen from other, equally successful ads or
salesletters. All 'great' copywriters do this. They steal. They
recycle. They copy. They model. They swipe.*

And they adapt.

*Of course, they must not be copied literally. (There's a big
difference between plagiarism and modelling.) But they can
be easily adapted to fit the market, the offer and the message.
I have a large swipe file that contains copies of ads, websites,
direct mail pieces and salesletters I come across. I then turn
them into templates or 'fill-in-the-blanks' formulas.*

*Study and model successful copywriting as much as you
can. Dan Kennedy, my mentor and a hugely successful
copywriter, teaches his students this exercise: buy tabloids,
such as The National Enquirer, on a regular basis. Of course,
the publication may be questionable for some, and it may not
necessarily fit with your style or cater to your market.*

But here's the reason why.

*Ad space in tabloids is excruciatingly expensive. If an ad is
repeated in more than two issues, preferably copy-intense ads
or full-page advertorials, commonsense tells you that the ad
is profitable. Rip out the ad and put it into your swipe file.
(If you don't have one, a shortcut is to copy someone else's, or
swipe from proven list of successful headlines.)*

*Then, copy the headlines into a document. They can be easily
converted into 'fill-in-the-blanks' formulas. And believe me,
they work well with almost all markets. I've tried these types
of headlines on both low-end and high-end clients, from
simple $10 products to six-figure investment opportunities.
And they worked quite effectively in both situations.*

The cosmetics of a headline is equally important if not more so. The type must be bold, large and prominently placed, even written in a different font or typestyle. It must 'scream' at your readers. Don't worry if it's too harsh or too long. (My experience tells me that the longer headlines pull the most, even for professional clients or in conservative situations.)

Specificity is also quite important. The more specific you are with your headline, the better the response will be. Use odd, non-rounded numbers because they are more believable and pull more than even, rounded numbers. (In it's commercials, Ivory Soap used to say it's '99.44% pure.' Of course, that number is more believable than '100%.')

Whenever possible be quantifiable, measurable and time-bound. For example, you're promoting some 'how-to' marketing program. Don't say, 'Increase your income' or 'make money fast.' Words like 'income' and 'fast' are vague. Be specific. Say, 'How six simple sales strategies helped me stumble onto an unexpected $5,431.96 windfall – in less than 27 hours!'

The bigger the numbers are, the greater the impact is. If you say 'five times more,' replace it with '500%' (or better yet, '517%' or '483%'). Don't say 'one year', say '364 days'. The brain thinks in pictures, not numbers or words. Both terms may mean the same thing, but one looks bigger.

Using some of the triggers mentioned at the beginning, here are some examples of being specific with your headlines:

➤ *Nine jealously guarded techniques that...*
➤ *Here are 17 of my most prized recipes for...*
➤ *How I made $42,791.36 in only 11 days with...*
➤ *Boost your golf drives by 27 yards when...*
➤ *A whole new way to lose 45 pounds in seven weeks with...*
➤ *Marketing toolkit contains 35 powertools that...*
➤ *Follow these eight magical steps to...*

➤ *Read this 22-chapter, 376-page powerhouse...*
➤ *The 10 commandments of power positioning...*
➤ *Chop paperwork by as much as 47% when...*
➤ *Slash your learning curve by four weeks with...*
➤ *...and start using within only 33 minutes!*

My favorite headline formula is the 'gapper', which is based on the pain-pleasure principle. In sales, it's referred to as 'gap analysis'. (Dan Kennedy calls it 'Problem-agitate-solve'. That is, you start by presenting a problem, you agitate your audience by making the problem 'bigger', more significant and more urgent, and then you present your solution in the offer.)

With the gapper there's a gap between a prospect's problem and it's solution (or a gap between where one happens to be at the moment and where that person wants to be in the future). But many prospects either do not know there is in fact a gap or, because it is one, naturally have a tendency to ignore it. It's simply human nature.

So a headline that communicates the presence of such a gap – or one that widens it (which can also be accomplished through other components, such as a surheadline, subheadline, 'lift' copy, sidenotes or opening statements) – will likely appeal to those who can immediately relate to it (i.e. people within that specific site's target market).

Opening the gap or widening it helps to reinforce a sense of urgency in the mind. After the headline visitors will want to know how, by browsing further, they can close that gap. And the wider the gap is, the greater the desire to close it will be. Why? Because it appeals to stronger motives.

Abraham Maslow, the famous psychologist who developed the hierarchy of human motives, stated that the foundation of all human needs is our need to survive. Once satisfied, the next one is our need for safety. Our need to be with other people is next, followed by our need to feel appreciated. Finally, our need to be challenged is at the top.

The 'pain-pleasure principle' states that people either fear pain (and try to avoid it) or crave pleasure (and try to gain it). When given a choice between the two, however, pain is a superior motive. Our need to survive and feel safe, which are at the bottom of Maslow's pyramid, rule over all other needs.

So, a headline that instantly communicates a problem (i.e. a painful situation or a potentially painful one that may arise without the benefits of your offering) will have more impact. People who associate with the message will feel compelled to read more, which also helps to identify your readers – it isolates the 'serious' from the 'curious.'

You heard it before: there's a difference between 'needs' and 'wants'. When I work with plastic surgeons, I often tell them to use as a headline, 'Suffering from wrinkles?' That way, it pulls only qualified prospects into the ad because it appeals not only to people with wrinkles but also to those who suffer from wrinkles (i.e. they want to do something about them).

A web salesletter I recently wrote for Michael Murray talks about the fact that he is a college student stricken with cerebral palsy who's 'made it' online. The copy and most of the headers use some of the triggers I mentioned earlier.

Below is a brief list. Can you identify them?

➤ *SPECIAL REPORT! Want to cash in on...*
➤ *...But don't have a product or a website?*
➤ *How a 'Physically Disabled' Teenager...*
➤ *Earn a $2,000-to-17,000 Monthly Downpour of Dollars...*
➤ *...On a Shoestring Budget!*
➤ *Jealously guarded 'secrets' are finally revealed...*
➤ *Get your hands on dirt-cheap products to sell...*
➤ *You'll never have to create your own products!*
➤ *...Model after actual websites 'making it' BIG TIME!*
➤ *PLUS, for a limited time only, the next 500 orders...*
➤ *And if I can do it, I'm sure most 'abled' people can!*

Michael is a 19-year old with cerebral palsy. (I was moved by his story.) With his headline specifically, I used strategies to increase the attention factor. My biggest concern was the fact that people have become desensitised with opportunities of this nature. So, while I catered to people's emotions, I used Michael's disability as a psychological 'hook'.

Ultimately, ask yourself: 'Does my headline effectively stop people from scanning my web page, capture their attention and trigger their emotions in order to pull them into the copy?' More importantly, ask yourself, 'Does my opening statement beg for attention, arouse curiosity and genuinely cater to the motives and emotions of my market?'

If not, change your headline and try different ones. Sure, the change may be small and insignificant. But often the smallest changes can create the most dramatic changes in your results.

This article shows us there are two forms of ad types.

Trigger compulsion

This is where you connect with the reader through sparking an emotion and then compelling them to read further.

Pain pleasure

This is where you identify with the reader's problem (pain) and then present them with the solution (pleasure).

Ad creator worksheet

So for my product I have to come up with phrases that match each type of ad for each type of customer. I use the worksheet below to throw in suitable phrases or words that might be used in my ad. At this point I do not worry about the character restrictions set by Google. This is just a worksheet where I put my ideas down.

Customer category	Core motive	Personality	Trigger	Compulsion	Pain of potential customer	Pleasure to be gained by customer
Owner	To increase profit	Formal	Seven easy steps to increase profit. Revealed! Closely guarded secrets by PPC gurus. The five biggest mistakes. Learn how, educate. Understand.	Find out how I reduced my marketing budget by 72%. Increased ROI by 72%. 'Special report'. Find out now, success guaranteed. Master Google in seven days. Step by step, simple. Successful entrepreneur shows you how, millionaire businessman shows you how.	Profit decreasing? Losses increasing? ROI decreasing? Earnings decreasing?	Maximise profit easily, tactics, strategic, entrepreneur, businessman. Keep ahead.
		Informal	Tricks of the trade exposed. Be the envy of your competitors. Slash the learning curve. We've cracked the Google code.	Non-technical guy shows you how. No technical knowledge needed. Adwords for dummies. Idiot proof way.	Cash going down the drain? Profit taking a nose dive? Wasting cash on AdWords.	Easy, simple tricks, tips. Kept the bank manager happy. Kept my creditors at bay. Idiot guide.
Part owner	To increase sales	Formal	Seven easy steps to increase sales. Sales went up by 56% in seven days. Sales increased by £23,000 in one month.	Read how I made it work for me.	Not meeting turnover targets? Revenue budgets not being met? Not enough clicks? Low traffic? Great site – no visitors?	Get qualified leads, genuine customers.

Part owner		Informal	Super charge sales in seven days.	Secrets revealed. Get going in 30 mins. Start boosting in just half an hour.	Sales taking a nosedive? Not getting the sales? I need sales help? Not enough sales?	Hungry customers knocking down your door.
Part-timer	To increase costs	Formal	Seven easy steps to decrease costs.	Save money, reduce budgets. Easily understood.	Cost reduction, overhead reduction. Expenditure spiralling out of control.	Save up to 73% on Adword costs.
		Informal	I will reveal to you. Let you in. Join exclusive club. Adwords on the cheap. Dirt cheap. Adwords on a shoestring budget.	Save money with in 30 mins. Slash costs on Google.	Wasting too much cash?	Slash your AdWord costs in half.
In the industry	To increase knowledge level	Formal	Seven easy steeps to increase knowledge. Professionals, PPC industry experts.	Educate, understand, proessor, export, teachings, latest papers research.	Not enough clients? Bridge that experitse gap. Frustrated with the way AdWord works?	Structured course making you the expert.
	To inceace knowledge level	Informal	Master, learn, wise up, crack the system, beat the system, become a Google pro.	Help your clients. One day course. Share knowledge with clients. Back to basics approach to AdWords. Share ideas with AdWord community.	Adwords driving you mad? Crazy?	Next level above Perry Markshall's book.

Just let your mind run free. It's a landing ground for any idea, phrase or word you have no matter how stupid it sounds. Sometimes the more stupid it is the more noticeable it is to the potential customer!

Once you've got all your ideas down I suggest you print it out. You will need to refer to this when constructing your ad so instead of scrolling up and down it's best to have this print out in front of your computer screen when drafting your ads.

You can use this worksheet opposite to help you. You can find it at:

www.MassiveAndPassive.co.uk/worksheets.html

Once you have filled this in you can move on to constructing the ads.

1	2	3	4	5	6	7
Know your customers	Segregate customers	Cater for personalities	Cater for ad types	**Write ad**	Allocate search terms for each ad group	Test, monitor and revise

Write ad

I would say this is the hardest part of the exercise. It takes a lot of patience and creativity to come up with ads that attract attention. You need to have your Ad Creator Worksheet in front of you, a nice cup of tea and your creativity cap firmly *on*!

Here's what I came up with.

Again I have ignored character restrictions set by Google,

3
Ad Creator
(Worksheet 3)

Customer category	Core motive	Personality	Trigger	Compulsion	Pain of potential customer	Pleasure to be gained by customer
1						
2						
3						
4						

Customer category	Core motive	Personality	Ad Type	Ad 1	Ad 2	Ad 3
Owner	To increase profit	Formal	Trigger compulsion	*Straight talking businessman* Shows you how he cracked the AdWords system that made him millions www.selfemployer.co.uk	*Non-technical guy* Shows you how to master AdWords in less than seven days. Are you ready? www.selfemployer.co.uk	*My profits increased by 968% in 29 days following this idiot guide on AdWords.* www.selfemployer.co.uk
			Plain pleasure	*ROI plummeting?* Follow this idiot guide and watch ROI rise in less than seven days. www.selfemployer.co.uk	*ROI less than 10%?* Follow these seven easy steps to master AdWords – are you ready? www.selfemployer.co.uk	*Profits decreasing?* Get real customers to your site by perfecting AdWords. www.selfemployer.co.uk
		Informal	Trigger compulsion	*Adwords exposed* We've cracked the Google code. Idiot guide is behind this click. www.selfemployer.co.uk	*Multi-millionaire* Reveals the tricks he employed to crack the AdWords code. www.selfemployer.co.uk	*We've cracked it* Get on the first page for 5p per click. Adwords has been mastered. www.selfemployer.co.uk
			Plain pleasure	*Fed up being poor?* Idiot guide reveals the tricks of the AdWords trade. www.selfemployer.co.uk	*Wasting cash daily?* Idiot guide on AdWords reveals the tricks of the trade. www.selfemployer.co.uk	*Great site – no visitors?* Get traffic by following this idiot guide on AdWords. www.selfemployer.co.uk

Part owner	To increase sales	Formal / Informal	Trigger compulsion / Plain pleasure			
Part owner	To increase sales	Formal	Trigger compulsion	*Straight talking sales guy* shows you how he cracked the AdWords system that increased sales by millions www.selfemployer.co.uk	*Non-technical sales guy* Shows you how to master AdWords in less than seven days. Are you ready? www.selfemployer.co.uk	*My sales increased by 968% in 29 days following* this idiot guide on AdWords. www.selfemployer.co.uk
			Plain pleasure	*Sales plummeting?* Follow this idiot guide and watch ROI rise in less than seven days. www.selfemployer.co.uk	*Conversion rates less than 10%?* Follow these seven easy steps to master AdWords – are you ready? www.selfemployer.co.uk	*Sales decreasing?* Get real customers to your site by perfecting AdWords. www.selfemployer.co.uk
		Informal	Trigger compulsion	*Adwords exposed* We've cracked the Google code. Idiot guide is behind this click. www.selfemployer.co.uk	*Multi-millionaire* Reveals the tricks he employed to crack the AdWords code. www.selfemployer.co.uk	*We've cracked it* Get on the first page for 5p per click. AdWords has been mastered. www.selfemployer.co.uk
			Plain pleasure	*Fed up being poor?* Idiot guide reveals the tricks of the AdWords trade. www.selfemployer.co.uk	*Wasting cash daily?* Idiot guide on AdWords reveals the tricks of the trade. www.selfemployer.co.uk	*Great site – no visitors?* Get traffic by following this idiot guide on AdWords. www.selfemployer.co.uk

Customer category	Core motive	Personality	Ad Type	Ad 1	Ad 2	Ad 3
Part-timer	To reduce costs	Formal	Trigger compulsion	*Straight talking businessman* Shows you how he cracked the AdWords system that made him millions www.selfemployer.co.uk	*Non-technical guy* Shows you how to master AdWords in less than seven days. Are you ready? www.selfemployer.co.uk	*My costs dropped by 68% in 29 days following this* idiot guide on AdWords. www.selfemployer.co.uk
			Plain pleasure	*Costs rocketing?* Follow this idiot guide and watch adword costs plummet www.selfemployer.co.uk	*Costs rocketing?* Follow these seven easy steps to master AdWords – are you ready? www.selfemployer.co.uk	*Costs out of control?* Follow this idiot guide and watch adword costs plummet. www. selfemployer.co.uk
		Informal	Trigger compulsion	*Adwords exposed* We've cracked the Google code. Idiot guide is behind this click. www.selfemployer.co.uk	*Multi-millionaire* Reveals the tricks he employed to crack the AdWords code. www.selfemployer.co.uk	*We've cracked it* Get on the first page for 5p per click. Adwords has been mastered. www.selfemployer.co.uk
			Plain pleasure	*Fed up being poor?* Idiot guide reveals the tricks of the AdWords trade. www.selfemployer.co.uk	*Wasting cash daily?* idiot guide on AdWords reveals the tricks of the trade. www.selfemployer.co.uk	*Great site – no visitors?* Get traffic by following this idiot guide on AdWords. www.selfemployer.co.uk

In the industry	To increase knowledge level			Adwords community	Adwords forum	PPC community
		Formal	Trigger compulsion	Get all your questions answered by our expert members. www.selfemployer.co.uk	Community of AdWords users. Perfect your marketing skills here. www.selfemployer.co.uk	Get all your adword questions answered by our expert members. www.selfemployer.co.uk
			Plain pleasure	*Lack knowledge?* Follow this adword expert's guide and watch your clients' costs plummet. www.selfemployer.co.uk	*Can't keep up?* Join our AdWords community to keep ahead of the pack. www.selfemployer.co.uk	*Can't keep up?* Join our AdWords community to the benefit of your clients. www.selfemployer.co.uk
		Informal	Trigger compulsion	*Adwords For The Pro* Discover the advanced thinking in this specialised industry. www.selfemployer.co.uk	*Adwords think tank* Discover the advanced thinking in this specialised industry www.selfemployer.co.uk	*Adword experts club* Find out the latest thinking in this specialised industry. www.selfemployer.co.uk
			Plain pleasure	*Lack knowledge?* Search our AdWords database for the answer. www.selfemployer.co.uk	*Can't keep up?* Search our AdWords database for the answer. www.selfemployer.co.uk	*Can't keep up?* Join our club of experts so you'll always get the answer. www.selfemployer.co.uk

but I have tried to keep it brief. I will simply re-edit the ads once I'm in Google AdWords itself. Now I have followed the trigger compulsion and pain/pleasure methods quite religiously. This is because it *works*! So do not be tempted to deviate from this simply because you can't be bothered. If you've hit a mental block then simply switch your computer off and then come back to it. There is no point in rushing through an ad. What will happen is that your ad simply won't get clicked and your CTR will plummet.

I've tried to write as many different type of ads as possible, but you will notice similarities in my set of ads. The reason for this is it's damned hard to come up with 48 individual looking ads! I think my set of ads are different enough to result in different click thru rates.

Important message

Some ads will work and some will not.

➤ The ones that work we keep.

➤ The ones that don't we revise, completely re-write or delete.

This is dealt with in section 7, but it's important to note now. It is good to write ads that are significantly different to see which ones work. Then you can start narrowing the difference over time according to which ones do work.

1	2	3	4	5	6	7
Know your customers	Segregate customers	Cater for personalities	Cater for ad types	Write ad	**Allocate search terms for each ad group**	Test, monitor and revise

Allocate search terms for each ad group

For the ad to get clicked it has to appeal to the reader. If it's written in a way that appeals to you because of the way you are and the search term is in the ad then bingo! You have a very good chance of being clicked. So if I was a formal business person fed up with paying a fortune to Google and I searched 'AdWords profits' and my ad was written in a formal trigger compulsion format like:

Profits decreasing?
Get real customers to your
site by perfecting
AdWords
www.selfemployer.co.uk

they would see that every word they searched was in my ad. This is because Google display it in bold if it matches. This will direct the searcher to my ad. Then the searcher sees that I speak their language. There is mention of typical business terms like decreasing (instead of less) and profits (instead of sales or costs). The searcher will think that I have got what they want and speak their language.

Getting the keywords

So how do you get the keywords? It's a two stage process.

1. You generate popular keywords and phrases that are often searched.
2. You add words from your ad (where possible) with the popular keywords and phrases.

To get the popular keywords and phrases surrounding a subject you simply find out, using generic terms, what is being searched. You do this by cheating! I know a site where you type in a search term and it will tell you how many times this search term and related search terms have been searched for in the previous month.

Visit: www.MassiveAndPassive.co.uk/get-keywords.html.

Type in a generic term surrounding your industry and you'll get all the phrases that have been commonly searched. So in my example my industry is the pay per click industry. So common generic keywords will be:

➤ PPC

➤ AdWords

➤ marketing

➤ advertising.

This site generates 100 key phrases per term searched. The site came up with the following search terms and number of searches.

Keyword	Search volume	Keywords	Search volume	Keywords	Search volume	Keywords	Search volume
ppc	1,959	google AdWords	1,085	marketing	33,159	advertising	23,323
ppc campaign management	693	AdWords	946	internet marketing	23,749	online advertising	20,329
ppc search engine internet marketing	653	AdWords bournemouth google	272	email marketing	15,546	advertising agency	8,067
ppc search engine marketing	535	advertising AdWords	251	marketing jobs	12,771	free advertising	2,564
ppc management	475	AdWords dorset google	233	search engine marketing	10,767	internet advertising	2,210
ppa.org.uk ppc	472	AdWords marketing	190	web site marketing	8,361	holiday advertising	2,035

Keyword	Search volume	Keywords	Search volume	Keywords	Search volume	Keywords	Search volume
ppc program	451	AdWords account	188	online marketing	4,062	advertising jobs	1,665
ppc search engine	450	advertising AdWords google	188	direct marketing	3,872	pay per click advertising	1,627
ppc bid management	424	AdWords analyzer	184	internet marketing strategy	3,244	marketing and advertising	1,554
freeware ppc	250	AdWords management	158	network marketing	2,841	banner advertising	1,489
ppc appraisal	166	adword AdWords google secret	149	marketing strategy	2,665	internet advertising promotion marketing	1,147
ppc software	136	AdWords google com	148	marketing mix	2,480	advertising campaign	1,137
ppc search	113	AdWords affiliate	133	marketing agency	2,285	advertising gift	1,136
AdWords cash google ppc profits	112	AdWords analyzer review	133	affiliate marketing	2,097	advertising consultant	985
http avantgo. com ppc	84	AdWords business google homebased	130	email marketing leeds	2,058	advertising agency newcastle	916
ppc uk	70	AdWords autopilot back by google guarantee guide money step step	129	marketing consultant	2,032	advertising agency in newcastle	890
ppc marketing	68	AdWords business homebased	125	marketing plan	1,962	advertising agency newcastle upon tyne	886
ppc advertising	61	AdWords blog	124	internet marketing leeds	1,935	advertising company in marketing newcastle pr	885

▶

Keyword	Search volume	Keywords	Search volume	Keywords	Search volume	Keywords	Search volume
click management pay per ppc	57	google AdWords coupon	122	marketing and advertising	1,554	on line advertising	811
free ppc software	55	pay per click AdWords	121	business marketing	1,477	outdoor advertising	744
ppc regulation	53	google AdWords campaign	120	internet marketing consultancy	1,447	advertising company	713
engine ppc review search	52	google AdWords management	118	sms marketing	1,414	advertising maker model	668
avantgo ppc	49	AdWords definite google guide	117	marketing company	1,346	advertising agency uk	614
ppc 2000	47	AdWords cash google ppc profits	112	professional search engine marketing	1,344	advertising agency e mail	613
ppc download free	47	AdWords definite guide	112	managed search engine marketing	1,332	web advertising	606
ppc game	45	AdWords cmd com google login main select	102	sales and marketing	1,213	advertising internet marketing plan	601
ppc application	43	AdWords cmd com google login main promo select sourceid	87	marketing communi-cation	1,200	advertising slogan	572
ppc campaign	43	AdWords secret	82	managed search engine marketing services	1,167	business to business adv ertising	564
engine marketing positioning ppc search	40	AdWords click google pay per	77	internet advertising promotion marketing	1,147	advertising balloon	553
ppc online	40	google.com AdWords	77	field marketing	1,143	pay per click internet advertising	548
ppc pay per click	39	AdWords hint	77	database marketing	1,112	advertising standard authority	531

Keyword	Search volume	Keywords	Search volume	Keywords	Search volume	Keywords	Search volume
ppc worldwide	39	AdWords google.co.uk	76	marketing services	1,100	tv advertising	508
free ppc game	38	AdWords definitive google guide	74	bulk email marketing	1,085	advertising software	507
ppc world	37	AdWords bid google management	65	chartered institute of marketing	1,059	billboard advertising	490
dvd to ppc	35	AdWords help	64	search engine marketing company	1,052	advertising intelligence	475
ppc affiliate program	31	AdWords goggle	63	e marketing	1,033	advertising photography	473
bournemouth ppc	31	AdWords promotional code	61	marketing campaign search engine	1,001	advertising solution	471
dorset ppc	31	make money with google AdWords	60	web site marketing uk	998	advertising holiday home	466
other ppc search engine	31	AdWords google promotion	59	auction marketing	988	radio advertising	466
66.84.56.206 ppc test33.exe	30	AdWords google profit	58	internet marketing uk	952	advertising cost	455
overture ppc	30	AdWords google secret	58	search engine marketing services	950	web site advertising	451
classic compiler mac ppc	29	AdWords profits	58	marketing research	948	recruitment advertising	447
ppc download	29	AdWords google income making money	57	internet marketing consultant	936	newspaper advertising	438
ppc engine	28	google AdWords tip	57	web site marketing strategy	926	advertising agency london	437
yahoo messenger ppc	28	AdWords overture	57	marketing northumberland	918	business advertising	429

▶

Keyword	Search volume	Keywords	Search volume	Keywords	Search volume	Keywords	Search volume
overture ppc management	27	AdWords software	57	consulting engine firm marketing search	903	car advertising	419
pcp company	26	AdWords designer	56	internet marketing northumberland	899	direct advertising	415
ppc 2003 software	25	AdWords definitive guide	55	internet marketing newcastle	898	free car advertising	414
media player for ppc	25	AdWords expert google	55	company marketing newcastle upon tyne	891	advertising uk	412
ppc services	24	make money AdWords	55	web marketing newcastle	890	media advertising	400
ppc optimizers	23	AdWords ebook	53	advertising company in marketing newcastle pr	885	free online advertising	374
ppc techs	22	google AdWords free	53	web site promotion internet marketing	869	advertising standard	364
fraud ppc	20	AdWords google hampshire new	53	marketing jobs uk	849	television advertising	362
internet marketing online ppc	20	google AdWords login	53	marketing recruitment	829	advertising standard agency	361
realplayer for ppc	20	AdWords login	53	marketing software	822	advertising history	354
195.92.194 2005 ppc	19	AdWords mania	53	keyword marketing	816	advertising resource	339
ppc system tuning	19	AdWords definitive google guide review	52	marketing idea	807	direct response advertising	325
google ppc	18	AdWords generator page	52	internet marketing solution	807	promotional adv ertising	325

Keyword	Search volume	Keywords	Search volume	Keywords	Search volume	Keywords	Search volume
marketing online ppc web	18	AdWords google mastering	52	agency engine expert marketing search	771	advertising direct online	318
ppc advertiser	17	write google AdWords	52	internet marketing and software. com	764	subliminal advertising	317
ppc theme	17	AdWords select	52	marketing solution	743	advertising product	313
avi free player ppc	16	AdWords services	52	search engine marketing reporting	737	advertising desktop	309
linux ppc	16	AdWords technology	52	search engine marketing uk	728	advertising agency mail	306
ppc tip	16	AdWords google nashua	51	consulting internet marketing service	727	advertising customised	302
ppc traffic	16	AdWords google test	50	marketing week	721	advertising agency marketing	298
ppc consultant	15	AdWords tool	50	marketing magazine	697	advertising inflatable	295
free ppc theme	15	AdWords google introduction	49	sales and marketing jobs	689	free web site advertising	291
locum ppc	15	AdWords stats	49	graduate marketing jobs	687	mobile advertising	285
ppc magazine	15	AdWords tracking	49	email marketing agency	679	child advertising	282
ppc maximizers	15	AdWords ranking	48	strategic marketing	679	advertising sales jobs	279
wardriving ppc	15	AdWords tip	47	online marketing solution	676	aerial advertising	278
6mm ppc	14	AdWords support	46	e serve marketing	673	free business advertising	278

▶

Keyword	Search volume	Keywords	Search volume	Keywords	Search volume	Keywords	Search volume
ppc advertise	14	google AdWords promotional code	45	multi level marketing	658	advertisi ng poster	278
elite.exe ppc	14	AdWords yahoo	44	search engine marketing pro	655	commercial advertising	271
free ppc	14	adsense AdWords google	18	ppc search engine internet marketing	653	email advertising	270
media player ppc skin windows	14	AdWords london	17	email marketing software	646	free job advertising	264
real player ppc	14	AdWords google select	12	online marketing business	644	magazine advertising	264
ppc ricochet serial	14	google AdWords affiliate	10	marketing mba	644	advertising career	261
pcsolutions	14	AdWords from google profit	10	marketing your site to the search engine	635	jobs in advertising	261
2005 informant ppc serial	13	AdWords from profit video	10	article marketing submit	632	free internet advertising	256
elite ppc	13	AdWords google software	10	small business marketing	630	motorway advertising	256
viewsonic ppc cbl 001 usb sync cable for pc	12	writing AdWords	10	email marketing uk	630	free banner advertising	253
2.11 3 ce pda ppc running windows	12	AdWords ask jeeves	9	marketing consultancy	624	advertising AdWords	251
2003 ppc	12	AdWords from google profit video	9	online marketing services	621	advertising pen	251
convert dvd ppc	12	AdWords get google top	9	definition of marketing	607	advertising business economy marketing	241

Keyword	Search volume	Keywords	Search volume	Keywords	Search volume	Keywords	Search volume
engine marketing placement ppc search	12	AdWords google tracking	9	advertising internet marketing plan	601	advertising drtv	240
gps for ppc	12	AdWords bid highest	8	viral marketing	598	taxi advertising	239
marketing online placement ppc	12	AdWords definitive google guide marshalls perry	8	internet link marketing strategic	595	free holiday advertising	238
marketing online positioning ppc	12	AdWords from profit	8	internet marketing promotional site web	569	search engine advertising	237
2002 ppc	11	google ltd AdWords	8	online marketing strategy	568	mother advertising	234
acer palm pda ppc s60	11	AdWords google suchmasc- hinen werbung	8	creative marketing	561	subliminal advertising save	231
activesync connection detect ppc vb.net	11	AdWords faq free google	7	agency mailto marketing	560	advertising agency email	230
chinese ppc translation	11	AdWords google hitbots	7	relationship marketing	552	free web advertising	230
click fraud ppc	11	AdWords name park sedo	7	marketing product	545	advertising copywriting	227
download fax ppc sms	11	123 AdWords google	6	international marketing	543	advertising technique	222
free ppc trial	11	AdWords affiliate tip	6	marketing gift	537	small business advertising	219
girl ppc virtual	11	AdWords clickbots google	6	ppc search engine marketing	535	advertising rate	218
hp ppc	11	google AdWords voucher	6	digital marketing	531	graduate advertising job	209

▶

Keyword	Search volume	Keywords	Search volume	Keywords	Search volume	Keywords	Search volume
6 data loading ppc rifle	10	AdWords uk	6	engine marketing search specialist uk	531	free advertising uk	207
advantage ppc scientific	10	google AdWords uk	5	engine firm marketing professional search	527	classified advertising	203

Now with these 400 keywords and phrases the site has generated you simply cut and paste them for each ad group. You will find that maybe only 200 or so of them are relevant so only use the ones that are.

You can only include one keyword phrase for one ad group. In other words each keyword or phrase is mutually exclusive. No ad group can have the same keyword or phrase.

The way you decide which keyword or phrase goes with which ad group is based on what the keyword or phrase is. So if the key phrase is 'marketing consultant' then, considering that the phrase sounds quite formal, we would put that in the formal business owner category. It can go in either the pleasure pain or trigger compulsion ad group as the phrase doesn't jump out as suited to either ad type.

For the high volume and generic keywords and phrases I rotate these amongst my ad groups. I call these floating keywords and phrases. I allocate them to the ads that I think are the best. I could be wrong (and usually am) but you have to allocate them to somewhere. Part 7 deals with testing how well your ads are performing. The best performing ads soon get the floating keywords and phrases allocated to them as they will stand the best chance of attracting a click.

So in my example the keyword allocations would start to look like this:

Group	Ad 1	Ad 2	Ad 3	Keywords	
				Mutually exclusive exact matches and negative matches	Floating broad matches and phrase matches
1	Straight talking businessman Shows you how he cracked the AdWords system that made him millions www.selfemployer.co.uk	Non-technical guy Shows you how to master AdWords in less than seven days. Are you ready? www.selfemployer.co.uk	My profits increased by 968% in 29 days following this idiot guide on AdWords. www.selfemployer.co.uk	ppc campaign management AdWords management business marketing advertising consultant profit AdWords technical AdWords idiot guide AdWords master AdWords	ppc
2	ROI plummeting? Follow this idiot guide and watch ROI rise in less than seven days. www.selfemployer.co.uk	ROI less than 10%? Follow these seven easy steps to master AdWords – are you ready? www.selfemployer.co.uk	Profits decreasing? Get real customers to your site by perfecting AdWords. www.selfemployer.co.uk	ppc search engine internet marketing internet marketing strategy ROI AdWords AdWords customer easy AdWords	ppc uk
3	AdWords exposed We've cracked the Google code. Idiot guide is behind this click. www.selfemployer.co.uk	Multi-millionaire Reveals the tricks he employed to crack the AdWords code. www.selfemployer.co.uk	We've cracked it Get on the first page for 5p per click. Adwords has been mastered. www.selfemployer.co.uk	ppc search engine marketing first page AdWords first AdWords tricks AdWords crack AdWords click	Google AdWords

Group	Ad 1	Ad 2	Ad 3	Keywords	
				Mutually exclusive exact matches and negative matches	Floating broad matches and phrase matches
4	Fed up being poor? Idiot guide reveals the tricks of the AdWords trade. www.selfemployer.co.uk	Wasting cash daily? Idiot guide on AdWords reveals the tricks of the trade. www.selfemployer.co.uk	Great site - no visitors? Get traffic by following this idiot guide on AdWords. www.selfemployer.co.uk	ppc management AdWords waste ppc bid management AdWords trick trade reveal AdWords AdWords secrets	AdWords
5	Straight talking sales guy shows you how he cracked the AdWords system that increased sales by millions www.selfemployer.co.uk	Non-technical sales guy Shows you how to master AdWords in less than seven days. Are you ready? www.selfemployer.co.uk	My sales increased by 968% in 29 days following this idiot guide on AdWords. www.selfemployer.co.uk	ppc program marketing strategy AdWords sales AdWords turnover AdWords system	marketing
6	Sales plummeting? Follow this idiot guide and watch ROI rise in less than seven days. www.selfemployer.co.uk	Conversion rates less than 10%? Follow these seven easy steps to master AdWords – are you ready? www.selfemployer.co.uk	Sales decreasing? Get real customers to your site by perfecting AdWords. www.selfemployer.co.uk	ppc search engine AdWords perfecting AdWords perfection	direct marketing
7	Adwords exposed We've cracked the Google code. Idiot guide is behind this click. www.selfemployer.co.uk	Multi-millionaire Reveals the tricks he employed to crack the AdWords code. www.selfemployer.co.uk	We've cracked it Get on the first page for 5p per click. Adwords has been mastered. www.selfemployer.co.uk	ppc appraisal AdWords exposed	internet marketing

Group	Ad 1	Ad 2	Ad 3	Keywords	
				Mutually exclusive exact matches and negative matches	Floating broad matches and phrase matches
8	*Fed up being poor?* Idiot guide reveals the tricks of the AdWords trade. www.selfemployer.co.uk	*Wasting cash daily?* Idiot guide on AdWords reveals the tricks of the trade. www.selfemployer.co.uk	*Great site – no visitors?* Get traffic by following this idiot guide on AdWords. www.selfemployer.co.uk	ppc marketing AdWords visitors AdWords traffic search engine	marketing
9	*Straight talking businessman* Shows you how he cracked the AdWords system that made him millions www.selfemployer.co.uk	*Non-technical guy* Shows you how to master AdWords in less than seven days. Are you ready? www.selfemployer.co.uk	*My costs dropped by 68% in 29 days following this idiot guide on AdWords.* www.selfemployer.co.uk	ppc advertising	web site marketing
10	*Costs rocketing?* Follow this idiot guide and watch adword costs plummet www.selfemployer.co.uk	*Costs rocketing?* Follow these seven easy steps to master AdWords – are you ready? www.selfemployer.co.uk	*Costs out of control?* Follow this idiot guide and watch adword costs plummet. www.selfemployer.co.uk	advertising AdWords	online marketing
11	*Adwords exposed* We've cracked the Google code. Idiot guide is behind this click. www.selfemployer.co.uk	*Multi-millionaire* Reveals the tricks he employed to crack the AdWords code. www.selfemployer.co.uk	*We've cracked It* Get on the first page for 5p per click. Adwords has been mastered. www.selfemployer.co.uk	AdWords marketing pay per click advertising	advertising
12	*Fed up being poor?* Idiot guide reveals the tricks of the AdWords trade. www.selfemployer.co.uk	*Wasting cash daily?* Idiot guide on AdWords reveals the tricks of the trade. www.selfemployer.co.uk	*Great site – no visitors?* Get traffic by following this idiot guide on AdWords. www.selfemployer.co.uk	AdWords account	online advertising

Group	Ad 1	Ad 2	Ad 3	Keywords	
				Mutually exclusive exact matches and negative matches	Floating broad matches and phrase matches
13	*Adwords community* Get all your questions answered by our expert members. www.selfemployer.co.uk	*Adwords forum* Community of AdWords users. Perfect your marketing skills here. www.selfemployer.co.uk	*PPC community* Get all your adword questions answered by our expert members. www.selfemployer.co.uk	advertising AdWords Google	internet advertising
14	*Lack knowledge?* Follow this adword expert's guide and watch your clients' costs plummet. www.selfemployer.co.uk	*Can't keep up?* Join our AdWords community to keep ahead of the pack. www.selfemployer.co.uk	*Can't keep up?* Join our AdWords community to the benefit of your clients. www.selfemployer.co.uk	internet marketing consultancy	marketing and advertising
15	*Adwords For The Pro* Discover the advanced thinking in this specialised industry. www.selfemployer.co.uk	*Adwords think tank* Discover the advanced thinking in this specialised industry www.selfemployer.co.uk	*Adword experts club* Find out the latest thinking in this specialised industry. www.selfemployer.co.uk	AdWords analyser professional search engine marketing	online advertising
16	*Lack knowledge?* Search our AdWords database for the answer. www.selfemployer.co.uk	*Can't keep up?* Search our AdWords database for the answer. www.selfemployer.co.uk	*Can't keep up?* Join our club of experts so you'll always get the answer. www.selfemployer.co.uk	ppc software internet advertising promotion marketing	

I would carry on allocating the relevant keywords to each ad group which I thought suitable. This would be because either the search term was in the advert or the search term tended to the type of customer catered for in the ad group.

However these search terms are all what is known as *broad matches*. Google further refines search terms as either:

➤ broad matches
➤ negative matches
➤ phrase matches
➤ exact matches.

Let me define them for you.

Broad matches

A broad match means that anything that is searched containing *similar* words in the phrase in your ad will show. So using the example of a broad match for:

➤ marketing strategy
the following phrases searched will cause your ad to be shown:

➤ marketing strategy analyst job
➤ marketing strategist
➤ market strategy
➤ strategic marketing.

Now you may want the last three phrases to deliver your ad, but you may not want the first one to. This is because the person typing that phrase in is looking for a job rather than help with building their marketing strategy. To avoid attracting the wrong type of searcher you use what is known as negative matching.

Negative matches

Using the same example as above you would simply put a negative sign before the word job like this:

➤ -job

This means that anyone who searches for job with any of the words in ad will not show.

Phrase matches

Phrase matches mean that the sequence of words has to be correct for your ad to show. Other words can be included either side of the phrase, but the sequence of the phrase cannot be altered nor words added in between. You do this by putting quotation marks around the phrase. So for:

➤ 'marketing strategy'
your ad will show for the following search terms:

➤ marketing strategy procedure

➤ help me with my marketing strategy.

But it will not show for:

➤ strategy marketing

➤ marketing and strategy.

This is because the sequence has changed or words have been added in between the phrase.

Exact matches

Exact matches means that what is typed in by the searcher matches exactly with your key phrase. To do this you put square brackets round the phrase. So for:

- ➤ [marketing strategy]
  your ad will only appear if someone searches:

- ➤ marketing strategy.

Your ad will not show for anything else. It will not show for:

- ➤ marketingstrategy
- ➤ market-ing strategy

etc.

Using these tools

All these tools (negative, phrase and exact matching) help reduce when your ad is shown. But why would we want that? Well this improves your click thru rate. And as shown above the better your click thru rate the less you pay for the same ranking.

You have to look at where your phrases could be confused with another completely different (and therefore irrelevant) business or subject. So if you were a used bike retailer using the phrase:

- ➤ used bikes

your ad will show when someone searches for:

- ➤ bikes used in the 2005 Tour de France.

The person searching using this phrase will not be interested in your site and will not click thru even though you have been aired hence your CTR will go down.

So my keywords in my above list will be 'cleaned' up by using these tools.

Trade names and misspellings

This is an excellent way to boost your chances for getting your ad aired. You have to include:

➤ all trade names
➤ all misspelt trade names
➤ all misspellings.

So I would include all my competitors (found through Google!) and all conceivable misspellings. One of my competitors is named Perry Marshall so I would include the following search terms:

➤ Perry Marshall
➤ Perry Marshal
➤ Pery Marshall
➤ Perry Marshll

etc.

I would also include misspelling of the search terms used above such as:

➤ markting
➤ marketng
➤ intrnet Marketing
➤ advrtising

etc.

Hopefully you can see now that I would generate keywords and phrases, running well in excess of 1,000 targeted keywords being relevant keywords, phrases, misspellings and trade names. This is now our starting list.

Set bid price for each search term

I would set the maximum price for all search terms at the start and refine it later. Now what you set it at is up to you depending on what type of person you are. I like to set it high and really go for it to see if the idea works, whereas others set it low and increase it over time and others set it to get a certain ranking (usually 1 to 8 so they get on the first page). I reckon you should try it all out and see what you feel most comfortable with at the start.

Part 7 deals with the analysis of these keywords because, trust me, some (and possibly most!) will *not* perform.

1	2	3	4	5	6	7
Know your customers	Segregate customers	Cater for personalities	Cater for ad types	Write ad	Allocate search terms for each ad group	**Test, monitor and revise**

Test, monitor and revise

Okay, we've written 48 ads, come up with around a 1,000 keywords and linked it all together. We now need to see what's working and what's not. I would suggest you give it a few days before you start making any brash or wild judgements on what is working or not.

When you log in to your Google AdWords account you will be able to look into the campaign at the actual ad groups. What you need to do to determine whether it's working or not is to see whether the adverts have been:

➤ aired enough
➤ clicked enough.

1. Getting your adverts aired

So looking at your list of ad groups you will see:

Default bidos	Clicks	Impressions	CTR	Avg CPC	Cost	Avg p

> **Default bid** – this is the maximum cost per click (CPC) you are willing to pay for someone to click on your ad. This you would have set at the start.

> **Clicks** – this will be the number of clicks your ad has received.

> **Impressions** – the number of times your advert has appeared after someone has searched for one of your specific terms.

> **CTR** – the click thru rate (CTR). This is the number of clicks divided by the number of impressions expressed as a percentage.

> **Avg CPC** – the average cost per click. So this is the total cost of clicks divided by the number of clicks.

> **Cost** – the total amount you have spent on clicks.

> **Avg pos** – the average position your ad has appeared in. So if it is in position 1 to 8 it will be on the first page of Google. It's an average so it will be expressed to 1 decimal place.

So to determine whether your ad has been aired enough look at the number of impressions for each ad group. If you haven't had your advert aired at least 1,000 times in a week then either your subject has no interest, you do not have enough search terms or you are not bidding high enough. So rather than writing off your project straight away and saying there is no interest I suggest you increase the number of search terms first then increase the bids.

Increasing the number of search terms

You do this by repeating 'Getting the keywords' section in section 6 of this chapter or visit www.MassiveAndPassive. co.uk/get-keywords.html. You have to think of more search terms to add so that you have more chances of getting your advert aired. Not until you have 10,000 keywords linked to your ads can you ever say that you have enough keywords.

Increase the bid for all search terms

If you increase the bid amount you will sometimes increase your chances of getting aired as you may outbid a competitor and rise the rankings of your ad. This will cause your average position to rise and you will get aired more often. How much you have to increase it by is unknown as it depends on your competitors. Sometimes I just double my max bid for a day and see what happens. I like to find out if my idea is going to work quickly rather than playing it too tentatively and then flogging a dead horse. But this all depends on your budget. I have fallen foul of this and spent £232 in one day on clicks!

Doing the two things above, increasing the amount of search terms and increasing the bids, will result in more impressions. Once you're over the 1,000 mark we can then start making some revisions to the campaign. You should really aim for 1,000 impressions a day from then on in to really push your website. One of my websites gets over 200,000 impressions a day! This is because I have thousands of search terms, pay up to £1.27p a click and the subject is really popular, being property.

2. Getting your adverts clicked

As mentioned above this is all about relevance and the strength of your ad. I am going to assume you have eliminated all search terms that are irrelevant as it is quite obvious when a search term is not relevant. You must remove all search terms that are not relevant as this will reduce your click through rate, thus Google will charge you more for your clicks.

Now if your ads are getting aired but not clicked there is something wrong with your ad. What Google does is air your three ads per ad group and 'split tests' the ads to find the best performer. So at the start Google airs all three in rotation and at some point chooses a winner.

It may be obvious to Google which is the winner if after a few thousand impressions the same ad keeps on getting clicked. If this is the case then Google will just air this one as this is the one that makes Google the most money! They want users to click so you get charged and Google gets paid. A good click through rate for Google is 0.5%.

If it's not that obvious then it will air until they're able to do so. Google may never make a choice if they work all pretty much the same. So you have two choices:

1. If Google has chosen a winner then delete the other two ads and write similar or better ones and try to beat the performance of the existing ad.
2. If Google hasn't chosen a winner (because they're either all good or all crap!) then consider rewriting all or some of the adverts in a completely different way if their click through rates are less than 0.5%.

So if you are trying to beat the performance of an existing ad then I suggest keeping the structure and wording the same, but consider the following.

1. Change the capitalisation of the ad – you can capitalise the title from 'Save money here' to 'Save Money Here'

or change the display url from www.propertyhotspots.net to www.Property Hotspots.net. This can catch a user's eye for whatever reason.

2. Add or remove punctuation – consider adding or removing an exclamation mark, @ sign, # or whatever else you can think of that makes grammatical sense. So 'Save Money Here!' instead of 'Save Money Here' or 'Rated Number 1' instead of 'Rated #1'.

3. Consider changing one word in the advert. So try 'Save Cash Here!' and test that.

Only make one deviation from the top performing ad and see which performs better. So you can have your top performing ad and then two other ads with one alteration each from the best performing ad.

So for example if the following ad was the top performer:

> Save Money Here
> The best loan rates
> Available to home owners
> www.phfinance.co.uk

The other two ads trying to beat this one would be:

> Save Money Here!
> The best loan rates
> Available to home owners
> www.phfinance.co.uk

> Save Money Here
> The best loan rates
> Available to home owners
> www.PHFinance.co.uk

with the exclamation mark added in ad two and capitalisation in the display url in ad three.

If either ad two or ad three performs better, i.e. has a higher click through rate, this becomes the top performer and another alteration is made to try to beat this ad. Then all you ever do is try to beat the top performing ad.

Conversion rate and cost per conversion

Another clever thing you can do with Google AdWords is track a 'sale' from a search term. This is helpful because you can track which search terms perform better than others. For example you may have the search term 'blue widgets' so not only can Google tell you:

➤ how many times your advert appeared

➤ how many times someone has clicked on your advert

➤ the average cost per click

but also the following:

The conversion rate

This is the number of times that after someone has clicked from a single search term they have actually bought from your site. In other words the click has converted into a sale. So you may have had 100 click thrus from the term 'blue widget' and three sales might have occurred from those 100 visitors. This would equate to a 3% conversion rate. You also may have had 100 visitors from the search term 'red widget' and one sale might have occurred from these 100 visitors. This would equate to a 1% conversion rate. So you could compare the search terms and deduce that the 'blue widget' search term converts better than the 'red widget' search term as three out of every 100 click throughs from the search term 'blue widget' result in a sale compared to only one out 100 click thus for the term 'red widget'.

This is very powerful information. It means that you can bid higher for the term 'blue widget' because you know that it is three times more effective than the term red widget. So take for example that both blue widgets and red widgets give you a profit before advertising of £10 per sale you know that for every 100 clicks on blue widget you make £30 and for every 100 clicks on red widgets you make £10.

So to break even for blue widgets you can spend £30 per 100 clicks or 30p per click and for red widgets you can spend £10 per 100 clicks or 10p per click. So you can see that you can adjust your bidding strategy on the performance of the terms you choose based on how well they convert. In this example the term 'blue widget' is worth bidding higher than 'red widget' as it makes you £30 per 100 clicks compared to £10 per 100 clicks.

Cost per conversion

This means literally as it reads. This is the cost it took you in clicks to get one sale expressed as an average. So if you spent £200 on clicks and got ten sales then the cost per conversion would be:

$$£200 / 10 = £20.$$

So the cost per conversion equals £20. On average the spend on clicks to get a sale is £20. You can get this data over any time period by just adjusting the dates within Google AdWords, so you can track whether over a specific period of time has cost you more or less to get a sale.

This figure is very important as it can tell you whether you are spending too much to get a sale. For the same reasons as above if you are spending £20 to get a sale, but the profit on the item is only £10 before advertising, you are paying too much for the clicks because £10 – £20 = £10 loss!

So it is a good idea to monitor the cost per conversion for the last seven days and make sure it falls within your budget. Please note: gather the data for the last seven days because this will give you a decent average based on current sales. If you do it for the time since you began the data becomes less reliable because it averages it out over a longer period of time. Depending on the number of sales you get it may be that you can gather data for less than seven days (if you sell many items) or greater than seven days (if you sell very few items) so that you get a good sample size to make accurate judgements.

Where and how to set tracking up

The two statistics can be found in the last two columns on the campaign page after 'Avgpos'. Setting up this feature is very easy. You just have to add a little text at the end of the destination url and a bit of copied code on the 'success' page. It's very easy to do, and Google guide you through it and explain it in dummy fashion.

To do this go to www.MassiveAndPassive.co.uk/conversion.html.

The lazy man's guide to Google AdWords

I sometimes create a Google AdWords campaign in ten minutes just to see how well an idea is received. So if you cannot be bothered to do what I have said above then do this, it will take you ten minutes or so:

1. Create a new campaign which is keyword targeted, give it a name and name your ad group anything you like. Choose the language as English and choose 'countries and territories' as the customer location and click 'Continue>>'.

2. If you want to add countries other than UK then add them on this page and click 'Continue»'.

3. Write the advert with a punchy title and catchy text. When you add the URL make sure you use capitalisation, eg www.MassiveAndPassive.co.uk like I have with the M A and P and then click 'Continue»'.

4. Open another window and go to www.MassiveAndPassive. co. uk/get-keywords.html and type in a short keyword that is related to your site. So if you are selling soft cuddly toys then type in 'teddy bear' and click on the '>' icon to start the search. A list of 100 keywords will be generated.

5. Copy and paste the whole list into the page being currently displayed by Google in the other window. You may have to clean the list generated as it will have the number of searches next to each keyword. I usually go into word and paste the table there, remove the first column with the numbers and then paste the table of keywords into Google. Google allows you to paste tables in their keyword text area.

6. Go back to the other window and search for another generic term and repeat for as many keywords you can think of. So you may do 'soft toy', 'toys', 'baby toys' etc. *Remember*: You can never have too many keywords! Then add these keywords as before until you have a list of over 500 keywords. Once done click on 'Continue»' in Google.

7. Enter the daily budget of £1,000. Do not worry, you will never spend anywhere near that if you are bidding less than £1 per click. I recommend setting it at £1,000 because if you put the budget to what you really intend to spend your adverts get slowed (i.e. displayed less) when nearing your budget for the day because Google fear they'll exceed your budget if it's displayed normally.

8. Enter your maximum cost per click. A good figure I choose is 12p, but it all depends on your pocket; 12p is usually enough to get your advert displayed.

9. Click on 'Save Campaign' and that's it. Your ad will be live straightaway.

10. After a few days check how many times you have been clicked. If you haven't had many clicks then increase the number of search terms, increase the amount you are willing to pay for a click and try changing your advert.

Getting on Yahoo!, Ask, Bing and others

A question that should be springing to mind is – what about the other search engines? This is an excellent question. You have to ask whether it is worth advertising on the others. The answer to this is as always – it depends! It depends on one and only one thing: if it works on Google!

➤ If it does it *will* work on the other search engines.

➤ If it doesn't then it has a very high chance of *not* working on the other search engines.

So I suggest you make it work on Google as this is the largest audience you're going to get and Google is the easiest and cheapest way to get visitors to your site. Have a look at the split of searches performed on the top five search engines in the UK for the month of January 2010:

Search engine	Share
Google	71.4%
Yahoo!	14.6%
Bing	9.6%
Ask.com	2.6%
AOL	1.1%
All others	0.7%

So you can see that Google has almost a three quarters share of the market. If you make it work on Google then I suggest you advertise on Yahoo! second (which includes you in Ask as well) and then Bing third. The others are worth doing if you are trying to squeeze every sale out of the searching population, which may be applicable if you have only one product that you sell.

You need to evaluate whether it's worth trying to master a pay per click system over developing new products. I choose to develop new products, but others focus on their one or two products. Neither strategy is wrong or right! It will depend on you and where you want to take your website.

To find out how to get on to Yahoo!, Ask, Bing and the other search engine pay per click programs visit: www. MassiveAndPassive.co.uk /other-ppc.html.

6 | Capture Emails and Send Newsletters

Pages to consult in this chapter:

www.MassiveAndPassive.co.uk/word-to-pdf.html
www.MassiveAndPassive.co.uk/hover-ad.html
(password: ahuja)

I run a newsletter and I earn anywhere from £7,000 to £15,000 per month from simply sending out an email every day. The way you do it is in three stages.

1. Capture a visitor's email and build up a subscriber base of 15,000+

2. Send them an email to their inbox, prompting them to click onto your newsletter page which is part of your website.

3. Have a newsletter that has content, but more importantly affiliate links and adverts in the page.

1. Capture a visitor's email and build up a subscriber base of 15,000+

The way you capture email addresses is to ask for them! I think we've all seen websites asking you for your email to join up to their newsletter. The great thing is around one in seven people do volunteer their email. Especially if you can promise them something in return.

This is what works for me. I:

➤ create a report or free gift
➤ create a hover ad
➤ create a sign-up page to capture their email
➤ link it all together.

Create a report or free gift

You've got to give them something in return for them giving you their email. A free report, piece of software a document or whatever. I create a report in MS Word then convert it into PDF to make it look professional. Put headers and footers into the Word document to make it look pretty then convert to PDF. To convert a word document to PDF visit: www.MassiveAndPassive. co.uk/word-to-pdf.html.

Try to think of what would be useful to your visitor that you could create. It could be your top ten tips on..., the best places to find..., the seven steps to..., etc and then offer it as a free gift in return for their email.

Create a hover ad

I create what's known as a hover ad that drops down after the reader has been on my site for five seconds. A hover ad is like a pop up add that can't be blocked. It pops up after five seconds so this gives the reader some time to get an idea about my site. If they click away before five seconds then they would never be interested in giving me their email. If they stay longer than five seconds then it's possible they would.

The hover ad would drop down and say something like:

> Join my newsletter now and get my FREE report on the **300 most affordable areas** to live in the UK
>
> JOIN NOW

So this eye-catching advert will drop right in front of them while they are reading. Now some people find this annoying, but most don't. Especially if they are interested in your subject. They will look at your offer and think they could do with that report, and since all they have to do is give their email, it seems a fair trade-off. My research has shown one in seven people are willing to do this if your offer is compelling enough.

To create a hover ad visit: www.MassiveAndPassive.co.uk/hover-ad.html.

Once created you click on generate code and copy and paste both parts of the HTML code into your home page. The way you do this is to go to the home page text editor as if you were going to edit the text of the home page, click on the icon that looks like '<>' and then paste both bits of code at the top of all the code. Then click 'Save Page >>>'.

The JOIN NOW is a hyperlink to a sign up page which you create in the website creator. To do this you need to create a sign up page first.

Create a sign up page to capture their email

1. Create a new page by going to website/edit/pages and then create new page.
2. Tick 'normal page'.
3. Name the page 'Newsletter Sign Up'.
4. Write a small piece like 'Give us your first name and email and you will get the latest information surrounding...' in the text editor.
5. Then click on the icon that looks like a piece of paper with two red lines on it. When you hover your cursor over it it's called 'Insert Form'.
6. A subscribe box will appear with text entry fields for their first and last name and their email.
7. Click on 'Save Page>>>'.

That's it. You now have your sign up page. It will be called www.yoursite. com/newsletter-sign-up.html and this is what you have as the hyperlink for the 'JOIN NOW' part of the hover ad.

Link it all together

You create the ad in the hover ad software, link the JOIN NOW text to the sign up page and add the generated code to your home page. Now you need to add the report to the welcome email they get when they subscribe. This is how you do it:

1. Go to mailout/autoresponder and then click on 'change autoresponder configuration>>>'.
2. Check the html/text combo box and click on 'Next Step>>>'.
3. Add the following text after 'This is to confirm you have been added to my mailing list': 'You can download your free gift by clicking here' and then highlight 'click here'.
4. Then click on the icon that looks like a paper clip that says 'insert file' if you hover over the icon.
5. Click on 'browse' and then click on the report you have saved on your computer.
6. Once uploaded click on 'insert file'.
7. Then click on 'Finish>>>'.

Now when someone signs up they will be sent an email confirming that they have been added to your mailing list and there will be a hyperlink where they can download your free report.

It took me around six months to build a subscriber data-base of 17,000 and since then it has hovered around this number as the same amount of people subscribe as well as unsubscribe. This is because the website creator allows the subscriber to unsubscribe at anytime with one click (to comply with spam laws). So my list stays at a healthy 17,000-ish. I do not know how long it will take you to build such a list. I think my list grew very fast as it's quite a popular subject. You may grow one even faster than me, you just don't know. The great thing is a hungry list = lots of money. This is because they come back to your site, clicking all over the place. You will understand as I go on.

2. Send an email to their inbox prompting them to click onto your newsletter page which is part of your website

I want you to read the above title very carefully. I am not saying send an email for your subscriber to read. I am asking you to send your subscriber an email which encourages them to click again back to your website. There is a distinct difference. I see many newsletters that come straight into your inbox and they are all there to be read. You need not click back to the site as they have given you all the information right there in the email message. I want the subscriber to read my email message and click back to my site.

The way you do this is to follow these three steps:

A. Get the email opened up and read

The best way to do this is to always put the subscriber's first name at the start of the email subject. The way you do this is to put [[firstname]] at the start of the email subject line and the website creator will substitute [[firstname]] with the subscriber's first name which they told us when they signed up.

Also, have an attention grabbing subject line. So the subject line:

John, find out the seven ways to save on your tax bill

is better than

Find out more about your tax bill

because it addresses the person directly, namely John, and it tells him that we have found out seven ways he can save on his tax bill. This is a lot better and more likely to get opened compared to 'find out more about your tax bill'. I hope you can see why.

B. Write an enticing email message

So using the above example you would not tell them in the email the exact seven ways to save tax. You would say something like:

> Hi [[firstname]],
>
> Did you know [[firstname]], one of my friends was about to submit their tax return when I said let me have a look at it. I was amazed at what his accountant had left out. I made four simple adjustments and saved him £3,487 and it only took me four minutes to do!

So I would use the [[firstname]] substitution a couple of times and then tell a bit of the story, but leave most of it out, leaving them hungry to find out about the four adjustments that only took four minutes.

C. Instruct them to click on further

At the end of the message I would finish with the words:

'If you would like to find out more visit:
www.ahuja.co.uk/2212

Ajay'

So I would tell them exactly where to click if they wanted to find out more. Do not just put your link as sometimes people just scan read and will not understand to click on that link to find out more. Also only include one link per email message so as not to confuse the reader. And don't forget to include the http:// before the www, otherwise the link will not work.

So all the way along I am enticing them to open further. Firstly to open the email message and then to open the page where the newsletter is displayed. If you manage to do this then you are on the way to making some money...the next part is crucial.

3. Have a newsletter that has content, but more importantly affiliate links and adverts in the page

Once they arrive at the newsletter you've got to deliver what you have promised otherwise they will not open up any further newsletters from you. You also need affiliate links (which are links that once clicked you potentially get paid on) and adverts (which you get paid on every time someone clicks on them).

So you have on the page the following:

1. The actual article.
2. Affiliate links which are related to the article. In my example I have spoken about tax so I will have affiliate links about tax, accountants, tax savings, etc that I have signed up to. Please see Chapter 8.
3. Adverts which are displayed by Google. Please see Chapter 7.

To see an example of my newsletter with affiliate links and adverts please visit www.ahuja.co.uk and you will see my daily newsletter.

⎡7⎤ Add Adverts

Pages to consult in this chapter:

www.MassiveAndPassive.co.uk/AdSense.html
www.MassiveAndPassive.co.uk/heat-maps.html
(password: ahuja)

Google AdSense

If Google hadn't done enough to change the way we use the internet by creating Google.com and Google AdWords they just went another step further and created Google AdSense!

Google AdSense was started in May 2003 and it enabled website owners to display adverts advertisers from who had signed up to Google AdWords. It has revolutionised the way advertising is conducted on the internet. You no longer need to approach individual advertisers to get them to advertise on your site and implement some kind of payment system because Google does this all for you.

All you need to do is sign up, generate some code by pointing and clicking your mouse and then copying and pasting this code into your site. Then you will get an advert that looks like

Investment Properties

We source properties from £50k. Minimum yield 10% www.propertyhotspots.net

Ads by Google

appearing on your site.

Every time someone clicks on the advert (and you can have up to 12 of these on your site) you get paid anywhere between 1c and $100. Yes, that is $100. The most I have ever been paid is $19.50 (approx £10) but there are some serious internet marketers out there in niche industries (which they keep very hush hush) where serious amounts of money are being paid for clicks.

Google pays you a percentage of whatever the advertiser has to pay. So if an advertiser in the UK is willing to pay £2 for a click and their ad is displayed on your site and it gets clicked Google will give you a share of that £2, paid in US dollars. The exact share is a mystery to me because Google doesn't tell you how much you get. Nor do they let you choose what ads get displayed on your site or tell you what you are likely to expect to get from the ads. You only find out once someone has clicked on the ad and you see what you get paid.

This is one of the most frustrating thing about Google AdSense but also quite a challenging sport! You have no control over what is displayed on your site or what you get paid. This is all up to Google. The only choices you have are:

1. How many ads appear on your site
2. Where they appear
3. What colours the ads are
4. The content around the adverts

And that's it. This is why it is an art form. Subtle changes can yield massive results. Google gets robots to 'read' your site and guess what your site is about and then add adverts they think are relevant to your site. All you can do is 1 to 4 above to make the right adverts appear so you get paid well.

The way to profit from AdSense is to tweak points 1 to 4 above to get your Google ads clicked. When your readers click you get paid.

To access Google AdSense visit: www.MassiveAndPassive. co.uk/AdSense.html and you can open up an account for free. They will guide you (very easily) in creating an advert. All you need to do is choose the colours and the number of ads you want and Google generate the code.

Adding Google ads to your site

1. When you're in the website editor go to: website/edit/ pages and then click on the page to which you want to add the adverts.
2. When you are in the page editor click on the icon '<>' and then the HTML code will be displayed.
3. Paste the code from Google AdSense at the top or the bottom of all the code. Do not try to read the code. It is possible to make sense of the code, but for starters just add it at the top and the bottom.
4. Click on 'Save page>>>' and then preview the page by clicking on 'View' next to the page name.

You should now see Google ads on your site. If not repeat the copy and paste again as the website editor can sometimes be temperamental.

Adding a Google search box to your site

Instead of cicking on 'AdSense for content' click on 'AdSense for search'. Here Google will guide you through generating the code for your site by pointing and clicking. Once the code is generated follow stages 1 to 4 above and your Google search field will appear.

Now every time someone searches through your Google search box and clicks on a sponsored ad generated from the search you will get paid. Just have a think about that. Every time someone uses your search box you potentially stand to earn every time. Just imagine that if you could get a user to perform all their searches using your box then you stand to make a fair bit from this user. On average someone searches via Google three times a day, which equates to 90 searches a month. If they click on a sponsored ad 10% of the time, paying an average of 25c per click, then each user you have is worth 90 × 10% × 25c = $2.25. So if you can get 2,000 users to use your site then you stand to make:

$$\$2.25 \times 2000 = \$4,500 \text{ per month.}$$

Many people are going after this market and actually succeeding. This is because since the search results are generated by Google there is no loss of search quality to the user using your search box over Google's as they are exactly the same. So if you provide better content around the search box than Google (which isn't hard to do!) users will be tempted to put you as their homepage as you've got more of what they're interested in.

That's the basics of Google AdSense. if you do get confused with their really user friendly program Google AdSense has excellent help sections. The difficult part, which Google doesn't help you with, is helping you to get your ads clicked!

Don't worry. When I discovered Google AdSense back in early 2005 I soon got the hang of it. By February 2006 I was earning on average $500 a day. My record day was $2,302!!!!! I got so good at AdSense that I wrote an eBook about it and I still sell it for £49.95. But seeing I'm kind of a generous guy I thought I would include it in this book for *free.* It's called *No Nonsense AdSense* and it's all about getting the most revenue out of Google AdSense. So here it is...

No nonsense AdSense

A comprehensive guide on improving AdSense revenue.

➤ Introduction
➤ Section 1 Can I make money with AdSense?
Why Google AdSense?
What do I have to do?
Is this legitimate?
Playing with AdSense
The outcome
Why should I spend time on AdSense?
➤ Section 2 How to optimise and tweak AdSense
Should I blend in or not?
Which size ads should I use?
Any AdSense to avoid?
Using images to improve click-rates
Do affiliate links affect AdSense income?
When not to use these techniques
Ten key tips when designing your site
➤ Section 3 Google AdSense resources

Introduction

This eBook has been written with the assumption that the reader has a basic understanding and some experience of Google AdSense. The idea of this eBook is to make the reader aware of how small yet significant tweaks can greatly improve and boost the Google AdSense income from a content-filled website.

Section 1 Can I make money with AdSense?

Why Google AdSense?

Google AdSense, if used in the correct manner, can prove to be a very fruitful revenue generator for Google, advertisers and most importantly, provide a healthy income for you.

What do I have to do?

In simple terms, create a content filled website, insert some AdSense scripts into your code and put your site online. With the right marketing, and using our strategy for AdWords, you sit back and watch the pounds roll in.

Is this legitimate?

If you visit every other site say, you are more likely than not to see some AdSense strewn across the page. This is completely legitimate and as long as you comply with the terms and conditions of Google AdSense, you're completely fine!

Have you ever clicked on Google AdSense? I initially thought that hardly anyone clicks on these links, but I was wrong. Are you a clicker or not? Well, you don't need to answer that as there seem to be a lot of people who want to click in the Google links shown to them as visitors are interested in that product, be it insurance or pottery classes. However, it is highly likely that at some point during your surfing life you have clicked on a link whether you knew it was sponsored or not as you saw something that you, the visitor, got drawn to.

Generally it doesn't matter what type of website you have, AdSense can substantially increase your online profits. What we are doing with this eBook is informing you of ways to increase the revenue generated from Google AdSense.

We are assuming that you have basic knowledge of the set up of AdSense and shall not be going over these steps. If you want to re-read the basics of AdSense, what it can do for you and how to set it up, then please go to www.MassiveAndPassive.co.uk/AdSense.html.

Playing with AdSense

I am doing what you are doing right now with AdSense. This is why you are here. You have heard of people making hundreds or even thousands of pounds a week through online clicks and you just don't seem to be able to. I was there at one point during my initial try out with AdSense a couple of years ago, but using key techniques outlined in this eBook, you too can significantly boost your AdSense income.

It took me a good six months to realise that something had to be done. Enough was enough. For every pound I was spending, I was making a mere 8 or 10 pence. This would be fine if I had 10,000 visitors a week clicking through on AdSense, meaning I would make a shade under £10,000 a week, but I wasn't even getting 1,000 people coming onto the site, never mind clicking the AdSense links. So, in conjunction with setting aside whole evenings working on improving AdWords, I would also look at ideas on how I can make the AdSense more appealing once I had a visitor to the site.

The outcome

I know I and other so called experts on AdSense have a lot to learn from this fast changing technology, but spending a little time playing with AdSense and AdWords has improved my AdSense income from £3 a day to over £250 a day. This dramatic improvement comes with simple techniques that I will expose in this eBook. You do not need to spend hundreds or even thousands of pounds on an e-marketer who promises to get you on the first page of Google results.

Why should I spend time on AdSense?

The income I generate from AdSense pays for my hosting, the website maintenance, pays wages of some of my employees and leaves a little left over for me to reinvest elsewhere. At the start of my AdSense campaign I was making a couple of pounds a week. Now I make thousands of pounds a week and this is improving month on month. Sure, I'm not a millionaire from it, but if I can apply the same techniques over and over to a tried and tested method, then there's no reason for me not to command a regular six figure income from this in the near future. That's why it proves beneficial to spend some time perfecting your AdSense on your pages.

Section 2 How to optimise and tweak AdSense

Every other site has some Google AdSense strewn across it somewhere. When I say every other, I mean small business types.

Once you have registered for an account with AdSense, you will have to decide where you're going to put it. If the site is being built from scratch, then it's much easier to place your ads. If it's an older site that you have then it's OK, but will be a little more troublesome to incorporate the AdSense.

People have two different strategies to the general introduction of AdSense:

i. Making the AdSense blend in with the background like this site: www.phfinance.co.uk.

ii. Making it stand out somewhat (but not being overbearing or disorganised) like this site: www.propertysourcer.com.

The worst thing to do would be to paste the AdSense code randomly, as you'll end up with a really ugly site where it is blatant that you are just offering links/clicks/spam.

To get an idea of how to place the ads, Google has offered heat maps to give you an indication of how they think visitors will most gain exposure to the ads. Visit www.MassiveAndPassive.co.uk/heat-maps.html (Google Heat Maps).

Should I blend in or not?

Answer person A: yes!

This is a tricky one. I *generally* blend my ads in. This means that I try to make it look like it is part of the site, because it is! I want to make money for my advertisers, which means more money for me, so I try to make it look like the links are relevant to their interests. If they have typed in the relevant keyword on Google search, then they should find the ads of high relevance.

How do I blend in?

Three key points:

- **Lose the border** - this can be done by making the border the same colour as the background.
- **Correspond the text font to the font on the ad write-up** - you should also change the colour to fit in with the colour of the text.
- **Lose the url if possible** - this is completely legitimate and it only involves you choosing the right ad. You cannot make the colour of the url the same as the background

**Leabharlann
Chontae Ceatharlach**

as this is against the rules of AdSense. What you can do, though, is choose the 728 × 90 ad size (see below) and when you have four ads popping up, the url automatically disappears! Great!

Answer person B: no!

Some people think that the heading should always remain blue, and this is understandable. Why you may ask? Well, people have always associated the dark blue colour with a link. So if they are to click on something, it will be the one that stands out as a link through! I don't use this strategy, but it has proved beneficial for some.

Which size ads should I use?

Google has published a list of the highest performing ad sizes:

➤ 336 × 280 large rectangle

➤ 300 × 250 medium rectangle

➤ 160 × 600 wide skyscraper.

I generally put a 728 × 90 banner across the top and on the bottom. Even though this is not mentioned in the top three, *for me*, it has been the most profitable. Again, I reiterate how it is important to play around and keep an eye on your statistics. What works for some doesn't necessarily work for others.

The next best performing size for me is the 300 × 250 medium rectangle. I have in the past used the skyscraper, but it didn't work for me, and this is the reason why: My sites are full of content. Content means space. I felt I was wasting space using a 160 × 600 skyscraper, and this has been justified by the increase of my AdSense clicks.

Any AdSense to avoid?

In my eyes, and pretty much in everyone else's, yes, there is one that you should try to avoid. The 468 × 60 banner has become so apparent on the internet that it is claimed that users of the internet have developed a natural blindness to any 468 × 60 banner as we automatically register this shape and size of banner with advertisements. 'Annoying, non-releveant, spamming' 468 × 60 banner is what signals in our heads and we automatically overlook it. Very much like advertisements on TV when an ageing, over-tanned man in a grey suit starts talking about insurance or 'consolidating your loan', we tend to ignore it as we automatically register it as a crummy company with something sub-standard to sell. Whatever the scientific reasoning behind it, it is generally agreed that this option should be avoided and it is one of Google AdSense's lower earning banners.

Using images to improve click thrus

Have you ever thought about using images to correspond to the Google AdSense listings? This legitimate way of adding a bit of life to your AdSense is easily done on the 728 × 90 board which usually holds four ads like the following:

Investment Properties	Investment Properties	Investment Properties	Investment Properties
We source properties from £50k. Minimum yield 10%	We source properties from £50k. Minimum yield 10%	We source properties from £50k. Minimum yield 10%	We source properties from £50k. Minimum yield 10% Ads by Google

This is fine as it is, but once images are applied the vast improvement in click thrus is really significant. The idea is to relate your content, write ups and images to the advertisements that come up. You should note that sometimes the 728 × 90 board will hold three advertisements as opposed to four, but the latter is more the case than not.

!!! Extra tip !!!

Do you notice how the url disappears on the 728 × 90 board when four advertisements come up? Try it for yourself and see. This makes it look less like a blatant advertisment and when tied in with a relevant image, makes it a worthwhile click thru for visitors. It's not tricking anyone, nor is it illegitimate or against the rules of Google AdSense. It's just polishing the rough edges.

Investment Properties	Investment Properties	Investment Properties	Investment Properties
We source properties from £50k. Minimum yield 10%	We source properties from £50k. Minimum yield 10%	We source properties from £50k. Minimum yield 10%	We source properties from £50k. Minimum yield 10% Ads by Google

Can you see how this has improved the aesthetic appeal of the clickthrus? It really does have a great effect on them. Test it for yourself and see the improvements. The key remark is relevant images.

You should note that generic/non-trade images should be used and not images that correspond to a particular brand or a specific type of consumer based product as this will firstly distract the person clicking and make them wonder about the image for too long and, most importantly, you could contravene the regulations of Google AdSense.

Do affiliate links affect AdSense income?

(To find out what an affiliate link is go to page 154)

It depends. If it can spruce up and add content to your page, then it should not really be a problem as long as they are affiliate links that pay out. It is no good having a 336 × 250 placard on the site that gets you a £3 commission every couple of months. You need to either:

i. Review the affiliate link and choose a better paying merchant.
ii. Remove the link altogether.

What you do with the remaining space is up to you, but again, I stress: *content is crucial.*

A good way to see if the links are having a positive or negative impact is to take the affiliate link down for two weeks and see how your AdSense takings have changed for that page.

It also depends on what affiliate links you are using and whether they offer high click thrus. My site phfinance.co.uk is a site that offers financial advice and products to visitors. I get a good return on the affiliate links as they are finance related, which pay out highly for visitors filling out their loan applications, mortgage applications, finance tracking, credit card leads, advice online and so on. So what is important is what your affiliate links offer and if they *add relevance* to the site. The finance affiliates usually pay anything between £2 to £115 for each lead, and I usually get around eight to ten applications a week through this, amounting to roughly £250–£1,000 every week! So in this case, the affiliate links are definitely staying online.

When not to use these techniques

In my experience, AdSense doesn't generate the best revenue through the following situations:

i. Placed in forums

Why not you may ask? Well, it's not that they don't work, they're just not relevant. For example, if your forum is on holidays, then someone will be writing about car rental, holiday insurance, bikinis, flip-flops, sun cream, etc, the list goes on and on. In such a mish-mash page where anything is being discussed, AdSense click thrus will not be as high as the AdSense targets words on the page to match advertisers. With such varied topics going on, you will also get a wide variety of Google AdSense.

So you may ask, should I not bother with AdSense on forums? Yes, yes and yes! It takes two minutes to do and the ads do get clicked even though at a much lower click thru rate.

The tip I can give you is to use 728 × 90 leaderboard across the top of the page or maybe a 336 × 250 underneath a placard with 'latest forum postings' or something of that ilk.

ii. Your site does not conform to AdSense program policies

Anything that violates the agreement with AdSense or content that is not suitable to host the AdSense. This means that any content that promotes pornography, gambling, drug use or any illegal activity is unsuitable for AdSense use. You are also forbidden from using AdSense to promote alcohol, tobacco, counterfeit goods and other controversial products or services.

I strongly recommend you do not even try to violate their policy as they will switch your account off, keep your pounds and not let you reapply for an AdSense account. I have seen it happen to someone. They had a great idea, played about slightly with the code (which is another violation of Google policy) and they just booted him out *without* any explanation.

iii. Placed in blogs

It is really difficult to get paid on blogs. Many bloggers complain of the low CTRs. If you want to put it on a blog then remember that you can still use a blog as your online diary or journal, but nowadays it's more profitable as a commercial blog.

iv. Your website gets too much traffic

The basic AdSense program is geared for small-to-medium sites. If your site gets significant traffic, look into the Google AdSense premium service (http://services.google.com/ads_inquiry/ct).

v. The ads are simply unsuitable

Although Google does it's best to find targeted advertisements that are relevant to a page's content, sometimes that targeting fails and unsuitable ads are shown.

vi. You make more money by keeping visitors on your site

The fundamental premise of pay-per-click advertising is that you're willing to send your visitors elsewhere in return for some kind of payment. If AdSense is your only form of revenue then this is an acceptable trade-off. If, however, your site makes you more from other programs, you should consider whether or not losing some of your visitors to pay-per-click ads is worth it.

Ten key tips when designing your site

1. If you're not a professional designer, then great! This is fine, as you want to keep your site simple and easily editable. No fancy graphics or flash required.

2. AdSense operates better with static sites than dynamic sites.

3. Make your AdSense ads look part of your web page.

4. Text ads are better than image ads.

5. Make more than one site and see what type of site is the most profitable, then work around repeating this type of website.

6. Do not include AdSense on web pages with MP3, video, news groups, and image results. Also exclude any pornographic, hate-related, violent, or illegal content.

7. AdSense for search – you can use this for your site search, and you get a percentage of ad clicks. Not many people know this.

8. Use your AdWords account (or open one) to find out how much advertisers are paying per click for any given keyword phrase.

9. Find high paying keywords and build a website around them, using AdSense as your source of revenue.

10. Most of all, experiment with what you have!

Section 3 Google AdSense resources

The following pages about Google AdSense can be found at www.MassiveAnd Passive.co.uk/AdSense.html:

- AdSense homepage
- AdSense support
- AdSense glossary
- Google guide to AdSense
- Google AdSense terms of service
- Google AdSense types
- Google AdWords.

Examples of my AdSense built pages

- Finance website: www.phfinance.co.uk
- Property: www.propertyhotspots.net
- Investment: www.ahuja.co.uk
- Forum: www.phforums.co.uk
- Search: www.propertyinvestmentsearch.com

8 | Sell Other People's Stuff

Pages to consult in this chapter:

www.MassiveAndPassive.co.uk/middlemen.html
(password: ahuja)

Affiliate marketing

If you sell other people's stuff on the internet without any purchase of the physical product or service, no order fulfilment, no liability and no stock holding then you are both considered an affiliate. They are an affiliate to you (a merchant affiliate) and you are an affiliate to them (an advertiser affiliate). This is one of the most effective ways of making money on the internet and was the real trigger for me to see how easy it could be to make a lot of money very easily. There is very little for you to do other than *market* your *affiliates* hence the naming of this emerging industry of affiliate marketing.

Affiliate marketing is where you, the website owner, sell products and services of companies you have decided to affiliate with (partner up in other words) in return for a commission.

The reason why this industry has exploded over the last five years is because the whole process can be automated. To become a reseller of someone's goods or services in the past required an initial phone call, a few meetings, a draft contract and then a final contract agreeing the terms and conditions. This cost a lot of time and money in lost productivity and professional fees. Today you can affiliate with some of the big high street names like Comet, John Lewis, Lloyds TSB, etc with just a few clicks – honest!

How it works

These are the basics.

1. You see a product or service on the web that you wish to sell. So you look for the link on the site that says 'Affiliates', 'Affiliate sign up', 'Partner program', 'Make money with us' or something like that and click on it.

2. They will tell you what commission you can earn if you sell their stuff. If you like what they're offering you can click further onto an affiliate sign up form where they will ask you the basics such as name, address, etc plus also how you wish to get paid, i.e. cheque, direct transfer, Paypal, etc. So you sign up.

3. After sign up you are directed to a page which gives you your all important 'Affiliate link'. This is a unique domain name which is related to you. So for example if I were trying to affiliate with Vodafone then my affiliate link may look like www.vodafone.co.uk/aid=ajayahuja. It doesn't matter what it looks like, but it will be a unique domain so that Vodafone can identify where their visitors have come from.

4. You include this unique link on your website and when anyone clicks through your link, visits Vodafone's website and buys from Vodafone's website within a specified time (usually 30 days) you will get paid a commission.

To try to think of this visually: think of your website as a market stall. You have approached the Vodafone shop at the other side of the town to introduce potential customers for them and they said they will pay you £20 for every new customer who buys a phone. To identify your introductions they give you this pen which makes an invisible mark on people's clothing but can be seen by a Vodafone's special lighting. Your pen colour is unique so that if a person comes in their shop with your ink on their clothing and buys then Vodafone will send you a cheque for £20 because the sale is traceable back to you.

Now this is occurring like mad all over the internet. Your internet persona is probably covered all over in this invisible ink and you have no idea! There are affiliate marketers out there that have enticed you onto their site because they promise independent reviews of products (such as *Which*), promised to tell you where to get the best price (such as Kelkoo) or simply because you log in to your email on this page and something caught your eye and you clicked through (such as MSN). All these companies employ affiliate marketing tactics and are making a nice little income off your back!

So it's down to you to get some income yourself. I know exactly where to go to get affiliated with the biggest and widest choice of affiliates and only require one sign up. These websites are like middlemen to the people who wish to market the goods and services and the companies looking for people who they want to market their goods and services.

Visually it looks like this:

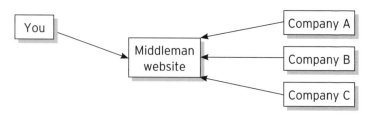

It's a big market place hosted by these middlemen where you can pick and choose who to be affiliated with.

The three commission types offered by these middlemen websites

The three types of commission you can earn from being an affiliate marketer are:

1. Pay per click.
2. Pay per lead.
3. Pay per sale.

1. Pay per click

Once you have obtained your unique link from these middlemen websites they will record how many clicks you receive on a daily basis. They will check that they are valid clicks to prevent click fraud (i.e. someone repeatedly clicking on your link) and will pay over whatever the agreed amount is per click.

So if you have this link on your website, and the agreed amount is 50p per click and you get ten visitors a day clicking on this link you will earn $10 \times 50p = £5$ per day. I will teach you how to get your affiliate links clicked further in the chapter, but I hope you can see that simply having a website with affiliate links can really deliver you a nice passive income. I mean, just imagine if you had 1,000 visitors a day clicking that link. That's £500 a day and trust me there are website owners out there who are making that and more from just one pay per click affiliate link.

2. Pay per lead

This is where a user clicks through your link and then fills out a form and clicks 'send' so that the affiliated site gets a lead. The form will usually at a minimum ask for their name, phone number and email. You get paid an agreed amount every time someone fills out this contact form and clicks on send. The affiliated site will then check the lead for authenticity by making contact, ensuring that the lead is genuine (so don't get ideas of sending the whole BT phone book because they will not pay out).

This is one affiliate link I promote heavily. I affiliate to many loan sites and they pay me up to £115 per authentic lead. Their criteria are that the lead must be over the age of 18, a home owner and looking to raise finance. If this is the case I get paid. I roughly get one in four leads approved and I have these links dotted about on my site. I reckon I earn about £3,000 to £4,000 per month from these links and all the payments go direct into my bank account. Now that's what I call passive! All I have to do is make sure my sites are live (by making sure I'm up to date with my credit card payments for the site) and I can be assured that some-one every day will click on one of those links so I get paid.

3. Pay per sale

This is where a user clicks on your link and actually buys on the affiliated site. So the user clicks on your link, visits the affiliated site, likes what they see and buys within a certain period of time. So they could visit the affiliated site, come away from it and come back seven days later, due to finding the site again, and buy and you will get paid. The only way you wouldn't get paid is if they found the affiliated site through someone else's affiliate link and not yours. The period of time is set by the website selling the stuff and is usually 30 days.

The sorts of commission you can get are a percentage of sale or a fixed amount per sale. Another exciting feature of pay per sale is that you can get lifetime commissions. So if the affiliated site offers 30 days tracking and a sale happens which results in the registering of a user and you get a percentage of sales of a user for life, then you can earn an income for life.

So, for example, this is a case that actually happens to me. I have several users who have registered on a gambling site through one of my affiliate links and I earn a lifetime commission on the profits on these users (i.e. the personal losses of these users) as long as they use this gambling site. I earn around £200 to £300 per month for this and I really do nothing because as long as they play (and lose!) I will still get paid no matter what I do. Just imagine if you had 1,000 registered users on a gambling site that paid out like this... you'd never have to work again!

List of middlemen websites

I'm sure you're itching to know where to find these middlemen websites aren't you? If not you should be! You can find all the middlemen websites at:

www.MassiveAndPassive.co.uk/middlemen.html

How to choose who to be affiliated with

There are only two rules you need to follow when choosing who to affiliate with.

1. The sites most relevant to your site.
2. The sites that pay well.

1. The sites most relevant to your site

If you have a site about French bulldogs then there is no point trying to recommend they open up a casino account with 888.com even if they do pay £100 per sign up! This is because your readers will simply be not interested in this because they come to you because of your information on French bulldogs. You may get the odd person interested in French bulldogs *and* in your offer of opening up a casino account, but the likelihood is very low and even though you might get a sale the amount of credibility you will lose will not make it worth it.

So in this example of a website about French bulldogs your readers would be much more receptive to you telling them about Direct Line's pet insurance which only costs £8 per month. They could sign up via your link and they will be unaware that for every click/sign up/sale you earn 50p/£2/£10 or whatever it is that Direct Line pay out. The conversion rate will be a lot higher than a gambling site!

This is why it is handy to have a site that you are personally interested in because you will have an intrinsic idea of what is of interest to your readers; you will have an understanding of their wants, desires and needs. If you know that vet bills are rising beyond inflation and you know that French bulldogs are more susceptible to infection, injuries, etc then pet insurance for vet bills will be a hot topic and well received. If you know rough costs of pet insurance to be £10 per month and Direct Line are offering £8 per month then you know that Direct Line's offer is cheap and will convert better. So really understanding your reader will help you choose the affiliated sites so that they get clicked and you get paid.

Since I am in the property investment game I know that property investors are interested in:

- raising finance cheaply and quickly
- finding cheap and below market properties
- money making ideas
- obtaining their credit file online.

I also know they are not interested in:

- gambling sites
- broadband and telephone call savings
- getting a deal on electrical goods.

Do you know how I know this? Because I have seen what has worked on my own sites and how much I've earned from having affiliated links for all of the things listed above. I too got tempted by the big commissions offered by gambling sites and realised that even though you get a few sign ups you don't really earn as much as if you did a proper targeted offer that is *relevant* to your reader.

I have around 20,000 subscribers on my property investment list and if I do a gambling promotion I might get one sign up which pays £60, but compare this to a loan promotion which pays £75 per lead where I might get 40 people making an application. So the gambling promotion earns me 1 × £60 = £60 and the loan promotion earns 40 × £75 = £3,000. So you can see how easy it is for me to decide what to promote and what not.

So browse the middlemen websites merchants' categories and see what categories would be of interest to your readers. Then look into the detail of what each merchant sells and think whether any of their products or services would be of interest. If so, sign up (if it pays well – see below), get your unique link, bung it on your site or newsletter and send out. If you add a sales pitch to it then even better!

Don't forget what I taught you in Chapter 3 about creating a sales pitch.

2. The sites that pay well

Let me explain this by way of an example. I was looking for an insurance site to market and I came across this insurance quoting site. Now I know that roughly 1% of subscribers to my property investment website would be interested enough in what I recommend to fill out an enquiry form or quotation form if I wrote a sales pitch about a particular insurance site.

So I looked at what this insurance quoting site was offering to affiliates and I was stunned. They were offering 1p for every quotation request regardless of if they take out the insurance. Wow wee! Let's say this insurance quoting site was super duper and 2% of my subscribers responded, then I could expect to earn:

$$2\% \times 20,000 \times 1p = £4$$

Now I don't know what your time is worth, but there is no way I could justify writing a newsletter about an insurance quoting website if all I could expect to earn is a few quid.

So I can hope you can see that you have to be affiliated with websites that pay a decent amount. The way you determine this is not as easy as it seems. In the above example you can see that there is no point in getting involved with a website that pays 1p per lead, but what about a merchant that offers £100 per validated lead where successful validation only occurs 1% of the time or £100 commission per sale where a sale only occurs 0.2% of the time?

The way you determine which sites pay out the most is by looking at the statistic 'Earnings per click', 'EPC', '7 Day

EPC' or something like that. The middlemen websites calculate how much the merchants pay out relative to the number of clicks generated by *all* affiliates over a period of time. So for example you could have two merchants, one offering £100 per validated lead, and the other offering £50 per lead and they both could have received 1,000 clicks over the last seven days from all the affiliates. Then compare this:

> Company A receiving 100 leads from these 1,000 clicks and paying out on ten of those leads of £100 each.

> Company B receiving 100 leads from these 1,000 clicks and paying out on 50 of those leads of £50 each.

We can deduce that the earnings per click are:

> Company A – (10 × £100) 1,000 = £1
> Company B – (50 × £50) 1,000 = £2.50

So we can see that even though Company A offers a headline commission of £100 per lead, a clear £50 higher than Company B, you actually earn more from Company B because they validate leads less strictly. So Company B would be the choice to affiliate with if they both offered the same product or service. What is to be learned here is do not get seduced by the headline commission. It's better to go with a merchant who offers you £1 per click/lead/ sale and pays out rather than a one who offers you £100 per click/lead/sale and pays out nothing! And trust me there are merchants out there who promise the world and pay out nothing, so beware.

This is also applicable for pay per sale. You may have the scenario where 1,000 clicks result in:

Company A receiving 100 sales from these 1,000 clicks and paying out commission on those sales of £10 each.

Company B receiving 200 sales from these 1,000 clicks and paying out commission on those sales of £10 each.

So the EPC would be:

Company A – (100 × £10) / 1,000 = £1
Company B – (200 × £10) / 1,000 = £2

So company B has a website that converts better than company A. It may be because it has a better sales pitch or a better product or service. Whatever it is you should promote Company B's website as the EPC is higher.

If there is no data on the merchant because they are new then look at what they are offering and see if it looks reasonable. For each type of commission consider the following.

Pay per click

This is fairly obvious to deduce. Either you like the amount or not! It's easily trackable so if they're offering you an amount that you're happy with then go for it. My threshold is around 50p per click. I would happily place a link on my site if the merchant would pay me 50p per click. Obviously it's a personal choice and you have to decide what you're happy with.

Pay per lead

Find out what they determine as a lead. If it is just their email address, and as long as it's a genuine working email, then it's likely that you will get paid as all they are asking for is a genuine email. So go to their website and if the form looks a simple one with a two-line form requesting the first name and email then it will be likely that you will get paid something. So as long as it's a decent amount they are paying, i.e. in excess of 50p or so, you can expect to potentially earn something from promoting their site.

If they determine a lead as someone filling out an eight page contact form asking their age, where they were born, their nickname at school and the size of their inside leg *and* only deem it to be a proper lead if they can contact the lead within five minutes of the merchant receiving the lead, then it is unlikely you will get paid. If there are too many obstructions to them paying out, like having too many questions or impossible contact times, then forget them. Stay away from these merchants as they are unlikely to pay out and all they want is free leads.

Pay per sale

If you are affiliating stuff relevant to your reader then the best test is to ask yourself 'would I buy it?'. If 'no' still ask yourself 'would I consider buying it under different circumstances?' like a different price, extra features, etc. If 'yes' then consider promoting it. You are the best acid test. If you would consider buying it then it will probably sell. Just because you think it's expensive or it doesn't do enough it doesn't mean that it is not attractive to someone else. Try to be unbiased about it and do not get seduced by the high commission rate. Step back and try to look at it realistically.

Not using middlemen websites

Some merchants (including me!) do not use middlemen websites. This is because they ask for too much of a cut or they simply have too high quality control procedures. In these circumstances you have to deal direct with the merchant themselves. This does not mean you have to speak to them or anything because you can sign up directly on their site. All you have to bear in mind, other than what has been said in this chapter is:

1. Check that the software they are using looks like it's going to track your sales. If they don't work you could end up promoting their site and never getting paid.

2. Keep track of who you sign up with. You will need to routinely check each individual merchant's affiliate login page to make sure they are paying out on your sales. Some affiliates can be really slow paying and sometimes they never pay. In this case remove your affiliate link immediately as you are promoting them for free.

Final note

Do not go overboard and clutter up your site with a load of affiliate links. Be selective. Go for the ones that convert, pay out and look good. Since you are associating yourself with these websites you need to make sure they're good ones with good customer support, easy to use, working websites and reliable. You are potentially putting your reputation on the line as you are endorsing their product so choose wisely.

Remember the saying: 'show me your friends and I'll tell you who you are'.

9 | Make your Site Sticky: Chat, Forums, Video Messaging, Latest News and Autoresponder

Pages to consult in this chapter:

www.MassiveAndPassive.co.uk/autoresponder.html
www.MassiveAndPassive.co.uk/forum.html
www.MassiveAndPassive.co.uk/chat.html
www.MassiveAndPassive.co.uk/news.html
www.MassiveAndPassive.co.uk/video.html
(password: ahuja)

Make your site sticky does not mean throw a load of jam all over it! It means make your site something for people to come back to. Think about what makes you keep going back to a site over and over again. The sites I go to over and over again are Google because they give you good search results, eBay because new items are uploaded every second for sale, Yahoo! because I log in to my Yahoo! mail account and Autotrader because I love looking at cars!

Now I can't show you how to create a search engine from scratch, build an auction site, create an email program or a database of secondhand cars, *but* I can show you how you can add pages to your site that keep users coming back because they have some degree of interactivity with them.

I call these 'hype it up pages'. And the great thing about these pages are they are completely automatic.

Hype it up pages

So why do I call them hype it up pages? Well they hype up your website! The pages that I will show you how to create are rarely found in most sites.

Most sites just sit there and remain static. Rarely changing, only ever changed if there is a change of address or phone number. They have the normal pages of who they are and what they do but that's it. They make no effort to give you anything more than just what they are about.

This is why the internet is wide open for success. The competition is just lame. It's usually some American nerd using a free website builder with lary colours with no idea of how to provide an easy to read, interesting experience to its visitor. When someone does create an okay site about a hot subject it isn't a surprise when it flies! This is because the creator has just gone that bit further in putting a bit of effort in so you keep visiting.

So the hype it up pages you should definitely include in your site are:

1. autoresponder
2. forums
3. chat
4. latest news
5. video messaging.

1. Autoresponder page

I love this page. It asks for the reader's first name and email and once given it will fire off one pre-written email a day *automatically* to the reader's email inbox for up to 365 days after they have given you their email.

So you could send an email:

- ➤ every day for 365 days
- ➤ once a week for three months
- ➤ every day for seven days
- ➤ once a month for six months
- ➤ every fourth day for eight weeks
- ➤ on the first day, the 52nd day and 245th day
- ➤ whatever sequence you want you can do it!

The difficult part is writing the damned emails. On my autoresponders I send an email every day for up to 160 days. Let me tell you, it took a long time to compile these. I do not expect you to follow suit.

The main message of these emails will be put on an individual page on your website. So the actual email they receive in their inbox will contain a brief message and then prompt the reader to click on www.yoursite.com/part1 which is a page you have created within your website with the article/newsletter/course section or whatever it is. Make sure you have all the AdSense adverts on these pages so that the reader has the chance to click on your adverts so you earn some dollars. I have run seven autoresponders and in the last three months they have made me over $10,000. And remember once set up it's automatic.

Below are some good ideas I have seen used and sometimes use myself.

'Get your free seven part course on...'

This is where you create a course or manual and split it into separate sections. In this example it's into seven. You could have the seven-part course on property investing and have part 1 as the formula, part 2 as raising the initial investment, part 3 choosing the right mortgage, part 4 as choosing the right property, etc.

So if you have a manual or course already written on something, or you know of a section of your information which tends to be presented as a course, then split it into x parts, create x pages with the info, link these pages to the emails to be sent out and then go attract some visitors to that page. And that's it. Anyone signing up will get your x part course on whatever over the period that you have set. So it could be your free nine part course on 'how to look ten years younger' sent by email every day for the next nine days.

Another trick is a few weeks after the course add some emails, then more every month or so with details tempting them back to your site. Or you could bombard them every day – it's up to you! Remember to use all the tips in Chapter 5 about writing emails that get opened and clicked.

'Join up for your free newsletter...'

This is where you make out that they are going to receive your newsletter as and when you prepare it, however it is newsletters that have already been prepared! If your subject is not too time sensitive then this trick could work. So if you were doing a newsletter on cooking with a recipe of the week you could send out newsletters with your latest recipes every week, but actually they're all your old recipes scheduled to be sent out week after week after they've given their email. The recipient would have no idea that the newsletters were pre-prepared because recipes of the week have no date stamp.

This method would not work for, say, the latest stocks and shares tips as these are very time specific because the info would be based on the analysis of current data.

'Give us your email and we will alert you when something suitable comes up'

This is saying something like 'register your interest here' or 'if you want to keep up to date with our latest develop-ments' etc. So you can send out irregular timed automatic emails to look like you're informing them of what's going on only when it happens. I've never used this strategy, but that's probably because my subjects never tend to this format. The sort of subjects that do would be ones where people just want to be alerted when something happens and they do not mind if this is every day for four days and then never again until eight weeks later.

To get an autoresponder page visit: www.MassiveAnd Passive.co.uk/autoresponder.html

2. Forums page

A forum page is where the readers of your website can communicate directly with each other. Many an online dis-cussion has occurred over the internet and there has even been a film made of one discussion about a young teenage lad in Japan requesting help to attract a girl he helped on a bus. The great thing about forums are that they require no input from you. The readers ask questions, pass comment or give advice by typing in messages known as 'posts' and these posts are displayed for readers to reply.

Think of a large room with hundreds of blackboards in it. The blackboards all have messages written in chalk on them, and when you enter the room you are given a piece of chalk and asked to comment on any blackboard story you like. There are also others in the room doing exactly what you are doing. Viewing the stories and commenting on the ones they wish to comment on.

I have a forum on my main site and I regularly read it. I learn a fair bit from it as I have experienced property investors who share their experiences of being a landlord, from which you can learn a lot. My forum page is the most visited part of *all* of my sites. I get around 5,000 hits a day on my forum page compared to 2,000 hits for my second most visited page, being my home page. So a forum page can be the biggest pull to your website purely because of the interactivity.

You can get a forum instantly by adding a forum page in the website creator, however the forum features are quite limited. To get a better forum page visit: www.MassiveAnd Passive.co.uk/forum.html.

3. Chat page

A chat page is where you can communicate in real time. So it's like a forum, but the messages are written right in front of your very eyes as the person types it! You may have heard about chat rooms. They're used heavily by kids and teenagers to meet up and chat about all sorts of things. It helped Yahoo! achieve some of it's success as it had loads of chat rooms. Even I used them in the past to have a laugh with other chat room users.

I have a chat room in all my sites which is actually one room linked to all sites. So if someone enters the room on one site and somebody else enters the room from another site they will be in the same room. I prompt my readers to enter the site at specific times to concentrate people entering the room at the same time to stimulate discussion.

The great thing about chat rooms is that they can keep people on your site for ages! If you like chatting then it is so easy for three hours to pass by without you realising. If your chat room has adverts around it isn't long before one of those ads catches their eyes and they click through, earning you money.

You can add a chat room to your site for free (if you don't mind having my logo and adverts on it) or you can have your very own custom chat room without my adverts but with your adverts. If you have your own adverts, you can have:

➤ four rotating text adverts at the bottom of the chat room
➤ a message with a hyperlink posted in the chat room every 1/3/10/30 minutes
➤ a logo at the top which can be a link to a site of your choice.

Try my chat page for starters and you'll see my adverts and how they work. If you want your own then you can copy my style of adverts for your own chat room. I'll show you how to do this in my site. To get your own chat room visit: www.MassiveAndPassive.co.uk/chat.html.

4. Latest news page

You can add the latest news from Google news, Yahoo! news or MSN news for the subject of your choice by simply copying and pasting some code into a page. The page updates automatically and can even display pictures from the story. Google, Yahoo! and MSN allow you to do this as the story listing contains a link back to their news site so they are happy for you to display their news.

You have to choose the news search term to get the relevant news stories. So for my first time buyer site, which is all about helping young people get on the property ladder, I have a page called 'latest news' and all the stories on this page have the following search term in the article somewhere: 'first time buyer mortgage UK'. This way I know I am going to get news stories about first time buyers in the UK and they will be related to mortgages. This way I avoid stories about first time buyers anywhere outside of the UK, and stories about first time buyers concerning anything other than property because I have included the term 'mortgage', so I avoid stories about first time buyers in the USA and first time buyers of cars.

To get your latest news page visit: www.MassiveAndPassive. co.uk/ news.html.

5. Video messaging page

This is a new thing which I reckon will replace forums one day. You can actually add a video forum (which looks like an ipod to me) to your website by copying and pasting some code in to your site. Then visitors can:

➤ add their own video recording of their message to your site

➤ send a video from their mobile to your site

➤ upload a video file to your site

➤ reply to whoever posts a video message on your site.

If you don't have video capabilities you can just add a video message.

I have one on my site and even though the concept is brilliant – no one uses it! I don't know whether it's because property investors are shy or simply because they do not understand how to use it. If I had a teenager site where young people were the users of my site I know they would jump onto it, but because it's just too new it hasn't worked...so far. The thing is it costs me nothing to keep on my site, but it will be there for my visitors to use when it becomes more mainstream.

To get a video forum completely free for your site visit: www.MassiveAnd Passive.co.uk/video.html.

10 Get Others to Sell Your Stuff

You know how I told you that you could sell other people's stuff in Chapter 8? Well this is the other way round. You get others to sell your stuff. This means becoming a merchant and finding affiliates to perform affiliate marketing of *your* product.

Remember I told you about middlemen websites that let you browse merchants, sign up with the ones you like and pay out in one go? You can't use these if you want to be a merchant. The reasons why are:

➤ They have too high quality control procedures.

➤ They require your site to have:

    – no adverts

    – no direct contact information

    – no affiliate links to any other site

    – no links that take you anywhere other than your site.

This is in breach of what I tell you to do all the way through this book. The reason for the disparity is because these middlemen want sites that are attractive to affiliate marketers. Affiliate marketers do not want to send visitors to a site, where the visitor can easily click away from the site, but the site gets paid by pay per click or affiliate links. Nor do they want the visitor to go direct to the contacts page and make a sale direct, thus cutting the affiliate out of the sale. Nor do they want it to be easy for the visitor to leave the site because they want you to stay on the site for as long as possible as you will be more likely to buy.

This is why the sites I recommend you create are affiliate unfriendly for these middlemen. However creating an affiliate program that cuts out the middlemen is attractive as you will get the smaller, less fussy websites marketing your site because it's very relevant to theirs. Only once you get to a certain level (say turnover £5m) should you consider grooming your site for these middlemen sites or creating an 'affiliate friendly' site alongside your own site for the middlemen websites to market.

Setting up an affiliate program

In the website creator I've told you to use there is a section called 'e-commerce'. Click on that and then go to 'your affiliates', then 'configuration' and then 'edit configuration now'.

You will be prompted for level 1 commission, level 2 commission and the affiliate home page. Let me tell you about these.

Level 1 commission

This is the commission you pay someone if they make a direct sale from promoting your product. So if you sell something for £100 and you set level 1 commission at 80% then the affiliate will earn £80 for every sale you make that has been referred by them. I like to pay out highly on level 1 as it encourages affiliates to market your product. I mean think about it – would you prefer to market a product that returns you £80 per sale or £8? So try to tempt them in this way and this will get you more visitors to your site and possibly more subscribers to your newsletter.

Level 2 commission

This is the commission you pay someone who has referred you someone who is going to sell your products. In other words you have referred a referrer! Then level 2 commission is the percentage of the referrer's commission payable to you. I set this at 10%. So for example if Joe had a site with my affiliate link and I was paying 80% on level 1 and 10% on level 2, and Rob clicked through Joe's link, signed up as an affiliate to my site and Rob made some sales resulting in £800 commission then Joe would be entitled to £80. This is because Joe is entitled to 10% of whatever Rob earns in commission.

The beauty of this is that you may recruit an affiliate who is good at recruiting affiliates only and is just happy to receive the level 2 commission rather than rely on level 1 commission. Then you can have affiliates recruiting armies of affiliates with these level 2 affiliates sitting back while their sub affiliates do all the hard work. This is another way some people have made serious money.

Affiliates home page

This is a page that you need to create. It is where the affiliate goes to once they have signed up (I will tell you how to set up an affiliate sign up further down). This page should be focused only on how to help the affiliate market your product or service. The way to create this page is best shown by way of example. Here's how I help my affiliates promote my products and services.

Text links

I give my affiliates suggested text links to include on their website and then tell them to embed their affiliate link into the text link. So the text links I suggest are:

> <u>Learn how to turn £500 into £10m in 90 days</u>

> <u>Learn how to invest like a property professional</u>

> <u>Buy properties with no deposit – Proven Property Investor</u>
> <u>Shows You How</u>

> <u>Entrepreneur Ajay Ahuja shows you how to make £1m fast!</u>

> <u>Join the biggest property portal website in the UK for</u>
> <u>FREE!</u>

So think of some punchy text links that are eye catching and explain your product or service in very few words. Then tell them to embed their affiliate link into the text link.

Adverts

Some affiliates may want to include a whole load of text about your site so they would want a mini advert/article to put on their site. So give it to them on a plate! The adverts I offer my affiliates look like this:

> I came across this guy who had written ten books on property investment and started with only £500 but is now worth £10m. He gives a load of free info, tips, books and even a tenancy agreement. I've used some of his tips to make myself a few quid.
>
> Visit [YOUR LINK]. There's tons of information there so I'm sure you'll find something that will help you.

This advert lets them know that:

➤ I'm credible because I've written ten books on property investment.

➤ You can start with as little as £500.

➤ The information is free.

➤ You get a tenancy agreement for free.

➤ They have made some money out of what I had taught.

I think this site is one of the largest property investment sites around. It claims to have over 90,000 subscribers which as far as I can see seems to be the biggest. The forum is very active with plenty of little tricks and tips to help you profit from property investment. It's even got a live chat room where other investors meet at 1pm and 7pm every day. Definitely worth a look. Visit [YOUR LINK].

This advert informs the reader that my site has a high number of subscribers and there are plenty of like-minded investors' opinions on my site for them to browse. I also highlight the live chat facility which almost all property websites do *not* have.

If you're looking to stay up to date with the property market then this guy, Ajay Ahuja, reckons he can keep you fresh with all the latest hotspots in the UK. I've read some of his books so I know he knows what he's talking about. His last hotspot was near where I lived so I rushed over there quick time and he was right – there were some bargains!

Anyway he's worth a look if you're interested in high capital growth properties. Visit [YOUR LINK].

Again this advert reinforces my credibility because I have written some books on the subject of property investment and that they have followed my advice and profited from this.

> Last week I joined up to this guy's 'Quit The Day Job' email series. I have been hanging off each email since. There is a whole load of inspiring stuff in it especially where he identifies how his time when he did have a job was spent thinking about TIME! Rushing to get to work on TIME, wishing time to pass fast during work and slowing down after work. Great stuff. Can't wait to hear what he has to say about finding that true vocation...Visit [YOUR LINK].

This advert tried to identify with the reader's pain of going to work with the hope of triggering with the reader some kind of empathy. It also hinted that you could find your true dream job from joining up to this email series.

So write something that's like an advert or an article which highlights the benefits and features of your products or services.

Banner advertising

I give them graphical banners I create in MS Paint. If you have a bit of graphical know how then consider creating a banner that is eye-catching. I have to admit the internet is becoming immune to banner advertising, but some affiliates still swear by them so try to give them a banner or banners to download. I use this one:

TURN £500
INTO £10m

and link it to my www.powerseries.org website.

Article advertising

Some affiliates like articles to put on their site. So write a punchy, attractive article that gives the reader a lot of information and tips rather than writing it as a sales pitch. The article I offer my affiliates reads like this.

How I turned £500 into £10m

I started investing in property in 1996 with only £500 and now I own a property portfolio of 150 properties worth over £10m. I can already hear you – 'it was easier back then!' Ironically it wasn't. Let me explain a little more. The buy to let mortgage had just emerged when I first started with only a few banks offering such a product. The banks that did offer such a mortgage were unsure, as this was new territory for them so they used to knock back a lot of properties that I wanted to buy. It was only really in 2001 that the banks got to grips with the buy to let mortgage and hence I was really able to expand my portfolio of ten properties to now 150 properties simply by investing in hotspots.

It makes me laugh when I read in the press that buy to let is dead. Well of course it is in most areas! But in some areas it is still waiting to boom. These areas I call hotspots. In 2004 alone I bought 50 properties. I bought in Hull, Stoke on Trent and Grimsby. These properties are no longer hotspots, as they are too expensive now. I've experienced 100%+ capital growth in one year which is well received but halts my buying sprees.

I intend to buy 100 properties this year *even* though all the so-called property experts are saying we are heading for a crash. Therefore I am always looking for new hotspots in the UK.

At the beginning of this year, 2011, I bought a property for £12,000 and another property for £23,000. And yes, they were in the UK.

What if I told you I bought these properties without my money – would you believe me? Well it's true. I bought it with the bank's money not mine. They even paid my legal costs! I did not put in one bit of my savings to acquire these properties.

I am sure you are aware that the loans and mortgages market is an extremely competitive market out there. The banks are desperate to lend and it seems they're not too fussy about your credit history either! You've seen the numerous ads on the TV and the newspapers promising you a decision in minutes and a cheque in days.

Now just imagine if you managed to get ten or so of these properties. You would be looking at clearing around £2,500 per month anywhere between years one to year four. That's £30,000 a year. I remember when I used to earn that working as a professional Chartered Accountant for 50 hours a week. I now earn ten times that working five hours a week!

The key to making money out of property is *where* you invest:

- I don't care about the national price index, as this is too general.
- I don't care about Halifax or Nationwide's regional analysis of property prices, as this is too general.
- I don't care what the property press think about where prices are heading.

➤ I don't care about so-called property hotspots that are going to double in value due to a train station being built in eight years' time.

All I'm interested in are properties that make me money *now*. This means that after my borrowing costs there is some left over for me to spend. If the property grows in value then great, but if it doesn't then – so what? If I'm making money every month then the capital growth is just a bonus.

So what happens if the price goes down? Well again – so what? I'm not selling the property as the property makes me money every month. In fact if the price goes down I'll just buy more!

Start with nothing – just like I did!

I'm sure you've all heard the only way to get rich is by using other people's money – and this is very true. Do not believe that if you work hard and pay for everything with your own blood, sweat and hard earned cash you'll get on. That way is the mug's way. You'll be working till you hit retirement age and probably beyond!

When I first started, no one had heard of me and I raised £500 in a day. Back then that was a lot of money to me. I used this £500 to make my first investment. After I caught the bug I started asking for more! I started to ask for £5,000 and more and most would say no but some would say yes! OK, I had to pay it back, but with the investments I made I paid them back and made 20 times more. I'll show you how you can raise £000s easily and fast.

One thing you can be sure of:

Property values rise in the *long* term.

So not in one month, one year or even five years. But over a period of ten years or more. So if you are considering investing for a period of longer than ten years you can be sure that your wealth will grow.

So how can you lock in certain capital growth?

Well you can't! But you can make a damned good prediction that it will. Take those two properties I bought for £3,000 and £9,000.

How affordable are they? Do you think a first time buyer could afford to pay £3,000? I'm quite sure they could.

How attractive are they as investments? Do you think there are many investors seeking a yield of 100%? I'm quite sure there are.

So if I were to try and sell this property I would get interest from both first time buyers and investors. So what would each of them be willing to pay?

Well the first time buyer could afford four times salary – so this would equate to around £60,000.

The investor would be interested in the property if it yielded 10% so this equates to £30,000.

So I could safely say the property is worth anywhere between £30,000 and £60,000 at some point in time. I would reckon three to four years.

▶

Notice I have not based the predicted price on *historical* growth patterns, as they are *irrelevant*. The past has nothing to do with the future when it comes to making investment decisions or predictions.

About the author

Ajay Ahuja is the owner of a buy-to-let portfolio of around 170 houses and flats spread across the UK. Visit his site [YOUR LINK].

Further marketing ideas for your affiliates

Apart from the ideas above you could suggest some other ideas on promotion depending on your product or service. Some of these below may or may not be applicable.

Type	Description
Newspapers	Place ads in free newspapers and magazines, local papers, tabloids and broadsheets. Classified sections would be a good place to put them as it will be cheap.
Email	Send an email to your friends list, work group list, your subscriber database or any other list you have. You could also tag it on to the end of every email message you send. Use the newspaper advert examples above. *Please note*: Do not spam. If you do not know the person and you've just got the email from a website then do not send as the email will get reported as spam and will not get through.
Website	Create a website and use your number and affiliate link as the only contact.

In person	Tell your friends, family, business contacts, work collegues, people on the street and whoever you come in contact with! You could get flyers made and hand them out or post them through people's letterboxes.
	If you're a member of a club you could give out these flyers to all the members or place a well positioned poster on the notice board.
Split your commission	You could offer to split this with another introducer. This could be anyone you know, a shopkeeper or simply someone you know who knows a lot of people.
	As long as you track the people they introduce there should be no problem in paying out commissions.
Post message on online forums	You can mention my services on money making or property forums and informally tell them about my services. You could also add at the bottom of your messages the newspaper adverts mentioned above to generate interest.

So use all of the above information from text links, adverts, banner advertising, article advertising and further ideas form the affiliate home page to which you make the landing page after an affiliate signs up. This way they can get straight in to promoting your products and services because you've given them the tools to do so.

Adding an affiliate sign up page to your site

When in the website creator go to:

1. 'Website', then 'edit page' then add a new normal page and call it 'affiliates'.

2. Then write a sales pitch about becoming an affiliate. If you want ideas then look at my page at http://www.ph finance.co.uk/make-lb10k-per-month.html.

3. Then write 'sign up now' or something like that on the page, highlight it and then click on the link logo that looks like ∞.

4. Then click on the link that says 'link to new affiliate form'.

5. Then the 'sign up now' text will be a hyper link to a sign up form which potential affiliates can click on to and sign up.

6. Then click on 'save page>>>'.

7. Then create another page of 'affiliate panel' type and call it 'affiliate login'.

8. Then click on 'save page>>>'.

You now have an affiliate sales page which convinces potential affiliates to sign up, a sign up page hyperlinked to the phrase 'sign up now' and a log in page where affiliates can check their stats and performance of how well they are selling your goods.

That's all you need to do to create a system where visitors can come to your site and start selling your stuff *automatically*.

My final thoughts

What I have talked about in this book has taken me two years to learn. If I were to split the time between researching and actual learning time I would say I have spent half my time finding out what to do and the other half teaching myself how to do it. If you are truly determined to make money on the internet and you are starting as a complete novice then you can start making serious money by year one. If you've got a bit of experience with using online software then I reckon you cut that time down to one month if you work at it and are not afraid of trying out new things and changing the model when it's not working.

The internet is moving and growing at such a fast pace that there is new technology coming out that is making routine tasks easier and easier. It's applying these technologies that benefit others that makes money. I wish you every success with your projects. I know that if you've bought this book you're ahead of 95% of people. One day we will all be on the net and we will all have our own websites, just like mobile phones, but at the minute the market is wide open for some of us...to make a whole load of cash!

Good luck.

Ajay

Ajay

Index

Some other titles from How To Books

Start and Run Your Own Business
The complete guide to setting up and managing
a small business

Alan Le Marinel

Whether you dream of owning a corner shop
or starting the next High Street chain, there are
few more exciting prospects than starting your
own business. This book will guide you through
the whole start up process and steer you on
towards success. It will help with:

- Defining your business strategy
- Researching the market and setting the right
  price
- Writing a business plan and raising finance
- Recruiting and managing staff
- Forecasting, budgeting and accounting
- Buying an existing business or franchise

Recommended by the Sunday Times – Business

ISBN 978-1-85703-988-7

The Small Business Start-up Workbook
A step-by-step guide to starting the business
you've dreamed of

Cheryl D. Rickman

An up-to-date approach to self-employment and
business start-up, this workbook shows you how
to research your business idea, plan the right
marketing strategies and manage effective
teams. It offers a selection of:

- real-life case studies
- practical exercises
- checklists
- worksheets

Other well-known entrepreneurs reveal what
they would have done differently, what their
biggest mistakes have been and what they've
learnt: Dame Anita Roddick, Julie Meyer,
Stelios Haji-Ioannou, Simon Woodroffe and
others expose their best and worst decisions and
contribute their tips for succeeding in business.

ISBN 978-1-84528-038-3

100 Ways to Make Your Business a Success
A resource book for small businesses

Neil Bromage

'Avoid those pitfalls and hit big time.' – *Sunday Mail*

'No waffle, no preaching, just straightforward advice written in an unfussy, no bulls..t manner. What a nice change.' – *K. Trimble, Gaelkat Ltd*

'The book is a valuable source of factual information that can be utilised in local and nationwide businesses.'– *The Gazette*

ISBN 978-1-84528-135-9

Getting the Builders In
A step-by-step guide to supervising your own building projects

Leonard Sales

Aimed at the lay client, this book gives practical step-by-step insight on matters that even experts in this field frequently fail to appreciate. Project management is partly about methodology and partly common sense. This straightforward guide is a refreshing approach to a diverse subject and keeps both of these factors in perspective.

ISBN 978-1-84528-233-2

Setting Up & Running a Limited Company
A comprehensive guide to forming and operating a company as a director and shareholder

Robert Browning

'Gives you all the essentials of how to form a business.' – *Working from Home*

As a chartered accountant formerly in public practice with many years' experience of small businesses, Robert Browning has set out simply how to decide whether a company is right for you and, if so, how to go about forming and operating it.

ISBN 978-1-85703-866-8

Investing in the Student Buy-to-Let Market

Ajay Ahuja

In this book buy-to-let guru Ajay Ahuja applies the same formula that has taken him from an initial investment of £500 to a portfolio of over 100 properties worth over £6m in less than five years. He will help you to; find the initial investment; find the right lender; find the right property; find the right tenant; minimise tax and operate legally.

ISBN 978-1-84528-008-6

The Buy to Let Handbook
How to invest for profit in residential property
and manage the letting yourself

Tony Booth

'An excellent first purchase for anyone
contemplating investing in the buy to let market
whether they are proposing to manage the
property themselves or to use an agent to do it
for them. First class and good value for money.'
– *The Letting Centre* (*Letting Update Journal*)

'An excellent piece of work that clearly and
concisely encapsulates the fundamental issues...
I will be seeking that the book is placed high on
recommended reading lists.' – *Philip R Gibbs,
Life President of the Residential Landlords
Association*

ISBN 978-1-84528-102-3

How To Books are available through all good bookshops, or you can order direct from us through Grantham Book Services.

Tel: +44 (0)1476 541080
Fax: +44 (0)1476 541061
Email: orders@gbs.tbs-ltd.co.uk

Or via our website
www.howtobooks.co.uk

To order via any of these methods please quote the title(s) of the book(s) and your credit card number together with its expiry date.

For further information about our books and catalogue, please contact:

How To Books
Spring Hill House
Spring Hill Road
Begbroke
Oxford OX5 1RX

Visit our web site at
www.howtobooks.co.uk

Or you can contact us by email at
info@howtobooks.co.uk